SEX EDUCATION:
A GUIDE TO EVALUATION
OF MATERIALS

WITHDRAWN

Second Edition

Janet Newman and Anthony Tilke

Youth Libraries Group
of The Library Association
1989

Youth Libraries Group

c/o Central Children's Library
Chamberlain Square
Birmingham
B3 3HQ

c. Janet Newman and Anthony Tilke, 1989

THE CONTRIBUTORS

JANET NEWMAN
  was compiler of the first edition of *Sex Education*. Previously librarian at Small Heath School, Birmingham, she is currently Senior Lecturer on the Women and Work Project at Coventry Polytechnic. She has written the general introduction and the introduction to each section.

ANTHONY TILKE
  who has compiled and annotated the items in this selection has worked for Hertfordshire Libraries and is now Assistant Borough Librarian (Young People's Services), London Borough of Havering.

CONTENTS

INTRODUCTION

Introduction

THE LEGAL AND POLITICAL FRAMEWORK

In this introduction I want to look at changes in legislation, in the political control of schools and of the curriculum, in the moral climate surrounding the controversy about sex education in schools and then proceed to consider the implications for those involved in the selection and provision of sex education materials.

The basic legal framework for sex education is laid down in the Education Act 1986, the provisions of which were circulated to Local Authorities in the D.E.S. circular 11/87 *Sex education at school*. This is concerned with two sets of issues: who should be responsible for sex education in schools and the moral context in which it should be placed. Governing Bodies are charged with responsibility for formulating sex education policy in schools, after consultation with the headteacher and others and with advice from the L.E.A. Excepted from these provisions is the teaching of sex education as part of an examination syllabus (e.g. Biology).

The guidelines state that sex education 'should present facts in an objective and balanced manner so as to enable pupils to comprehend the range of sexual attitudes and behaviour in present day society, and to make informed, reasoned and responsible decisions about the attitudes they will adopt'; at the same time it should be taught in a way which has 'due regard for moral considerations and the value of family life'. (DES circular 11/87, based on the Education (no 2) Act, 1986). Children should be taught what is and is not legal, and the guidelines forbid teaching which presents homosexuality as the 'norm'.

The Education Reform Act of 1988 further removes curriculum control from L.E.A.s through the establishment of the 'core curriculum' of basic subjects. Areas such as 'personal and social education', in which much sex education has taken place, are likely to suffer as a result. The Local Government Act of 1988 is also relevant in that it says that a Local Authority shall not promote homosexuality, and shall not teach it as a pretended family relationship.

These provisions are limited, but the effects of the legislation are potentially wide-ranging, partly because of uncertainty and fear on the part of sex educators. Sex education has become something of a political football in the attacks on local authorities by central government; for example, the furore about the 'positive images' policies on homosexuality of some London Labour-controlled councils was orchestrated at the time of the May 1987 local government elections which preceded the general election, and fed into the construction of images of the 'loony left'. Books played an important role here, with the fuss about *Jenny lives with Eric and Martin* but this perhaps said more about political manouevering than about the virtues of that particular text.

The focus on sex education also feeds into attacks on teachers who have become scapegoats for what is perceived as the moral deterioration of society. 'Professionalism' is no longer seen as a positive criterion by society at large, and this has significant implications for us as librarians. The calls for greater accountability in the development of policies, in the selection of texts, should in many areas be welcome; however we must ensure that the criteria we develop as professionals are clearly articulated and fed into the general public debate. I want to look at three areas affected by recent legislation and try to untangle some of the issues.

DEVELOPING A MORAL FRAMEWORK

One argument often used by the moral right is that sex education encourages promiscuity — i.e. children will practice what they hear about. Interestingly, my own research on the development of sex education in the 1960's shows that this development took place partly as a *response* to fears about increasing promiscuity in that period. It was argued that the decline of religion among young people had left a moral gap; and rather than attempting to enforce traditional values of right and wrong merely by restating the moral injunctions, it was more effective to educate young people into the moral values of personal responsibility and to prepare them for marriage and family life through sex education in schools.

Most sex education in Britain is based on these values, and cannot be seen, therefore, as either amoral or immoral. However, rarely do we find specific moral injunctions of 'thou shalt not...'. The reasons for this are educational rather than moral. Carol Lee, writing about her experiences as a sex educator in *The Ostrich Position*, says

"*...education is not a programme of indoctrination but a long process of enquiry which depends on a child learning to think for him or herself. The word instil presumes that teachers are active in putting in and that pupils are passive receivers — i.e. empty vessels. Education in morality is vital, and it is crucial, therefore, that it is education and not indoctrination.... Parents often ask 'But how do you educate children without telling them what is right and wrong?' The broad answer is that good teachers seek to discuss issues with pupils so that they might learn to think things through for themselves.... It is people's fear that education equals indoctrination that causes so many problems*"

This suggests that as librarians we should be looking for books which follow this same technique — which discuss moral issues and provide young people with a framework for thinking through issues for themselves, which promote responsibility in behaviour towards both self and others, and which take account of the social contexts in which sexual behaviour takes place. At the same time we should be critical of texts which present sex as a purely medical or biological phenomenon, removed from its social and moral context.

CONTRACEPTION

In 1984 we saw the development of a battle between Mrs Gillick and the DHSS about the confidentiality of contraceptive advice to the under 16's. This was constructed by Mrs Gillick and the 'moral right' as a question of who was ultimately responsible for children — the state or the parent. The attacks on professional power were resisted forcefully by the medical lobby and by others such as children's rights groups. Interestingly both sides used civil liberty arguments to reinforce their position, one emphasising the rights of parents, the other of children; while the medical profession used social welfare arguments — the consequences of lack of contraceptive advice for girls from 'deprived' families — to counter new regulations.

In this case the moral right was not a clear winner; Mrs Gillick lost in court but won an appeal, while the DHSS eventually reversed this decision in the House of Lords. However by then the harm had been done — professionals, including teachers, no longer felt safe in providing contraceptive advice; and some books which did not make the legal position clear were withdrawn from some bookshops (e.g. Cousin's *Make it Happy*, which was eventually republished with a revised text).

Following the Gillick case there was some concern over the presentation of information on contraception to young people. Two points are important in deciding our policy here: the first is that we can make a distinction between the giving of *advice* on contraception to the under 16's (the subject of the legal wranglings between Mrs Gillick and the DHSS) and the provision of *information*; and the second is that, as the National Council of Women's Report comments, *"Most of the evidence...supports the conclusion that simple provision of information about contraception appears to have no direct effect on contraceptive practice"*.

IMAGES OF HOMOSEXUALITY

The Local Government Act, the infamous clause 28 of which forbids local authorities to 'promote' homosexuality, can be seen as a direct attack on the 'positive images' policies of some councils; but it was of great concern to librarians because of the possible implications for stock selection. Most legal advice suggests that the provision of information about homosexuality does not constitute promotion; however the depiction of homosexuality as a way of life equally valid to that of heterosexual marriage is more contentious — this is precisely why *Jenny lives with Eric and Martin* raised such fears.

The treatment of homosexuality is perhaps the biggest minefield we face at present. However the problem is not as great as it might at first appear. Going back to the legislation, it does not suggest that we should not teach young people about homosexuality, but that teaching should not advocate homosexual behaviour, present it as the 'norm', or encourage homosexual experimentation by pupils. (DES circular 11/87, based on the Education (no 2) Act 1986). No mainstream sex education titles that I have seen, do any of these. Most texts adopt one of three approaches to the topic: the first is that homosexuality is deviant behaviour and homosexuals are to be condemned; the second that homosexuality is a pathological condition (i.e. a kind of disease) caused by medical factors, and homosexuals deserve our compassion; and the third, most common, depiction is that homosexuality is a 'stage' which most (male) adolescents go through, but which normal males grow out of to achieve maturity; homosexuality, here, is seen as an immature form of sexuality, or a form of arrested development.

These images have been condemned by the homosexual community and their criticisms have had some impact on some — a very few — sex education books. However this impact has *not* led to texts which actually advocate or encourage homosexuality. And we must remind ourselves of the limited effects of sex education, especially of books — homosexuality cannot be created by reading about it.

The difficulty for us here is balancing the problems of the current political climate, in which homosexuals are being scapegoated for many of the ills of society — social ills, as well as the physical threat of AIDS — against our professional values which seek to provide help and reassurance for young people who may be concerned about their own development. I feel that we also have a professional responsibility to counter some of the scapegoating of homosexuals by providing books which provide a historical and social perspective on homosexuality — good examples are to be found in Kaye Wellings *First love, first sex*, Suzie Hayman's *It's more than sex*, and Deborah Saunders *Let's discuss sex*. The latter also discusses the scapegoating of homosexuals in the context of scares about AIDS.

PROFESSIONAL VALUES IN THE CLIMATE OF FEAR

One of the worst consequences of the amount of debate and controversy surrounding the topic in the late 1980's has been the 'climate of fear' which has grown up, which has in some cases led to overcaution in our selection and provision of these materials. It is vital that teachers and librarians develop strong *professional* criteria which can guide their choices, rather than entering into the quagmire of moral argument. Each of us, of course, has our own moral views; however we need, I think, to be clear about our professional criteria so that we do not get drawn into fruitless debates over whether or not we should teach sex education or provide sex education materials. Instead we should be arguing about *what kinds* of materials we should be providing and how they should be used. Our selection criteria need to be clear, so that we can defend our choices and, equally important in the context of professional accountability, so that parents, school governors and others can enter into the debate.

DEFENDING THE PROVISION OF MATERIALS

Books have, in my view, become a mistaken target of attack since they are relatively unimportant in the formation of young people's values and behaviour. Farrel ('*My mother said*', 1978) found, unsurprisingly, that peer groups are by far the most important source of information and creator of attitudes. However, as we all know, peer groups can also be a great source of misinformation and can create, rather then dispel, anxieties in the young.

This means two things for us as librarians. Firstly, while books are comparatively unimportant as sources of basic sexual knowledge for young people, they do have an important role in helping both parents and teachers in their educational roles, and we might stress this more in our provision. There is a strong case for establishing 'parent and teacher' collections (which will, of course, need to be properly promoted, not regarded as an easy way out of the dilemma of what to put on the open shelves).

Secondly, however, young people do need private sources of information to check questions, to puzzle out things they have heard from their peers and to reassure themselves about their own development when they are made to feel 'different'. Books have an important role to play here and it is vital that they do not shirk difficult or controversial matters since it is in precisely these areas that clear information is needed. Easily accessible information — with A – Z formats and/or good indexes — should be an important criterion.

One strong argument for maintaining collections and supporting sex education teaching by the provision of materials lies in the findings of the Policy Studies Institute's survey on sex education in schools. This showed that most parents held positive attitudes to school sex education; most have a low opinion of their own knowledge and ability to convey that knowledge, and are glad for schools to take some of the responsibility. Furthermore, we have to take account of the gap between parents and teenagers which makes family based sex education problematic at an important age and of the argument that, given the incidence of sexual abuse, home is not always the safest place for young people.

GUIDELINES FOR PROFESSIONAL CRITERIA

Deciding on clear selection criteria is not an easy task since these will depend a great deal on the context in which we are working. Sex education materials, as well as being used directly by young people, are a highly mediated form of material — they are used by parents with their children, by teachers and youth workers with groups of young people, and by a range of professionals working with the young but wanting to improve their own knowledge.

Developing professional criteria in the current climate is a difficult business. However, it is essential that we stand outside the moral debate, and do not get drawn into responding to one moral position by articulating its opposite; we need to use the language of professionalism rather than of morality in defending our choices.

Finally as librarians we will no doubt be sensitive to any potential censorship from others, and may well go to considerable lengths to resist it. However we should also be conscious of the possible processes of self-censorship — of deciding not to handle some kinds of material in case it leads to problems, and consequently not making an important source of information available to young people, their parents and teachers.

In the set of guidelines which begins each section, I have looked at traditional stock selection criteria — vocabulary, level, illustrations and so on — in the context of the broader discussions about treatment and approach which are current.

Some of the general points I consider important are:

Linking biology to the social and moral context

* Books should encourage responsible attitudes and behaviour in relationships, and should provide young people with a framework for developing their own values and attitudes. This means a process of education, not indoctrination.

* Books should present sexuality in a moral framework, while acknowledging that there are variations in what is held to be moral in different periods, and in different religions and cultures. They should present morality not in terms of universal truths, but in terms of the social context of sex; responsible behaviour means taking that social context into account. We must provide, and be prepared to advise on, a range of approaches which different religious or ethnic groups will find acceptable.

* Books should make the law clear.

Clarity and relevance of information

* Books should provide clearly explained factual information about human development, reproduction and sexuality, rather than attempting to teach the subject indirectly through analogies with other species, or an overly depersonalised scientific approach.

* Books should provide information to give young people practical help, as well as moral guidance, in making informed choices about their sexual attitudes and behaviour. This includes information on contraception; on sexual abuse; and on 'safe sex' and AIDS.

Developing values and attitudes

* Books should encourage positive attitudes to oneself and one's sexuality, and should reassure the reader about the physical and emotional changes of adolescence. Positive representations of female sexuality are especially important for girls.

* Books should help overcome sexual myths and stereotypes rather than contributing to them, especially in the present climate of fear about homosexuality.

* Books should not distort reality for the sake of morality. They should not, for example, present a distorted or over-sentimental picture of the family or of marriage — there are important class and ethnic variations in both. Divorce, single and step parenthood and homosexuality exist and cannot be hidden.

BOOKS FOR YOUNGER CHILDREN

Books For Younger Children

This section includes titles for pre-school, infant and junior age groups, up to the age of puberty.

SEX EDUCATION NEEDS AND APPROACHES
1. Where do I come from?

At the preschool and infant ages the focus is on reproduction, and most books follow a 'Where did I come from?' structure. At the earliest stages books can help children learn about reproduction in the context of their own family, and many are produced in picture book format, to be shared by parent and child, around the birth of a new baby in the family.

2. Learning about the human body

However, as well as learning about reproduction, children need to grow up feeling positive about their own bodies, and getting the tone right is very difficult. *The Body Book* is a good example of a child-centred approach for junior age children. However where books have been produced for younger age groups (as in the *Child's playbook about sex*) they have usually failed because they have broken the conventions about childhood as a nonsexual, innocent state too dramatically or because particular parts of the book have been taken out of context by their critics. However this is still a real need in sex education for younger children. If, as it seems, it is not acceptable to present books directly to children which deal with their own developing interest in their bodies, then books for parents and teachers must attempt to address this subject.

3. Answering young children's questions

As the parental role and responsibility in sex education receives greater stress, and it becomes more problematic in schools, titles should be available which help parents answer their child's questions and deal with a child's inevitable interest in things she/he hears about sex as well as about reproduction. Children are sexual creatures from a very young age, have boundless curiosity, and while most people agree that difficult questions should be answered, how to do it is not easy.

14

SELECTION CRITERIA

Personal context

The context should be human, not animal, based. Human reproduction is different from animal, except in the most basic scientific details, and should be treated as such. Books which deal with both human and animal reproduction — those designed for primary schools, for example — should not use analogies with animals to get over the 'difficult bits', i.e. father's role, but should deal with human and animal reproduction separately.

We need more titles which follow the story of 'Where did I come from?' from a boy's point of view.

Family context

Reproduction and birth are social, as well as natural, events and take place in social contexts: usually a family. However, what kind of family is portrayed? Stocks should include titles which reflect the range and diversity of family forms, both in terms of class, ethnicity, and family structure, including some non-traditional forms. Adopted children also need to know 'Where did I come from?'.

Content

Most books for the early years use a narrative story approach around the story of birth. Things to look for in the narrative include:

— Is the mother or the embryo the main character? Lavish illustrations tend to mean too much focus on the development of the embryo, at the expense of conception, the mother's pregnancy, and birth.

— What is the role of the father?

— Is human intercourse included and if so, is it suggested that this is only a reproductive event? Some titles imply that conception takes place every time and that couples make love only because they want a baby.

Illustrations

In books for younger children these are very important to the tone and style and should be looked at critically not just for their content but in terms of the atmosphere and perspective they convey.

— Is the human body glamourised?

— Are sex and reproduction portrayed as aspects of 'science' (depersonalised technical diagrams) or, at the opposite extreme, are they over-romanticised?

— Where diagrams are included, do they divorce parts of the body from the whole? Young children's conceptual grasp may mean that they do not understand illustrations which show only part of a whole, and need to see how a picture of the embryo, womb, vagina etc relates to the body of the mother.

— What kind of images of the family and family relations are portrayed?

— Do the books show many more pictures of naked females than of males?

— How are 'difficult' subjects — e.g. birth itself — represented?

Vocabulary

Obviously this needs to be clear and simple for young readers; but books should use simple versions of the 'correct' terms for parts of the body (penis, vagina, womb) and sex (make love, have intercourse) and avoid animal based analogies (nests instead of womb, mating instead of intercourse).

Level

We need titles at a range of levels of detail and difficulty — learning about reproduction is not a single event, but should follow the child's curiosity at different stages of development.

ALEX, M. and B.
Our New Baby.
Lion, 1982, 0 86760 357 7.

Set in the context of young children enquiring and exploring bodies and reproduction, this title explains very simply how a new addition to a family arrives. Colourful photographs show a familial setting — in this case a Christian one — where two young children await the arrival of a new sister/brother. The parents explain simply about conception and we are taken through the stages of pregnancy and birth. This is done adequately, but conception is seen as a reproductive act only and there is little indication that sexual intercourse can be a beautiful and enjoyable experience in itself. Also, the diagrams used divorce the sperm, foetus and womb from the female body, so the whole context is not seen. The photographs show a fairly idealised background and the family is nuclear and middle-class, thus limiting the points of experience for many children.

Nevertheless, this will satisfy several questions asked by young children and the information is presented in a comforting way. The text is easily read and understood, and uses proper medical terms. The book treats the new arrival as another relationship the children must adjust to and enjoy as life progresses, and provides a Christian perspective for young children.

Age: 3 – 6.

ALTHEA.
A Baby in the Family.
Dinosaur, 1981, 0 85122 284 6.

Set in the context of a loving relationship between parents, this book is designed for young children who want to know exactly how a baby is born. The clear illustrations and simple but accurate text show the stages from conception to birth with the parts played by each partner. The medical terminology is properly used, although Althea suggests that family words for male and female organs are used at first and correct terminology used later.

Age: 3 – 5.

ALTHEA.
The New Baby.
Souvenir Press, 1973, 0 285 62120 3.

Intended for very young children who are about to get a sister or brother, this seeks to explain very simply that a mother gives birth to a baby.

Conception is not covered, nor really the father's role, but with its clear, colourful illustrations and simple text, this can be used as an introduction and may help to alleviate sibling rivalry.

Age: 2 – 4.

BALDWIN, Dorothy and LISTER, Claire.
Safety when alone.
see CHILD SEXUAL ABUSE

BOSCHE, Susanne (photographs by Adreas Hansen).
Jenny lives with Eric and Martin.
Gay Men's Press, 1981, 0 907040 22 5.

Originally published in Denmark, this book concerns Jenny, a five year old, who lives with her father (Martin) and his friend Eric. A brief text supplemented with many photographs takes us through their weekend, including a visit from Jenny's mum, gardening, playing games and visiting the laundrette. It is from here that the three bump into a neighbour who calls Eric and Martin 'you gays' in a derogatory manner. Upon enquiring why Mrs Andrews is angry, Martin and Eric draw a cartoon story to illustrate very simply how two men may have a loving relationship and want to live together, which some people in society may disapprove of — through ignorance, the book believes.

Objections to this book are based on the fact that it presents homosexuality as a normal, valid lifestyle, rather than as a deviation. These objections are out of all proportion to the book's availability and use, and form the focus of attack on some local authorities' positive images policy. In the light of the fuss, this title should be dealt with carefully, but the book at least does present, through the cartoon story part, a good response to a young child's question, when curious about the term homosexuality, which is a difficult concept to explain.

The total book is over-long and the story laboured, in order to make a point. The photographs are black and white and look uninteresting — some librarians have pointed out that the format mitigates against its use — it looks as if it ought to be located in a kinder-box, whereas some would feel this to be an inappropriate place. It should be noted that several library authorities have purchased a copy of this title, but have located it in a collection under the control of a librarian for use in special needs circumstances.

Age: 4 – 7.

CONLON, E.
Where do I come from?: A sex education book for young children.
Ard-Bui, 1984 (2nd edition), (O/P).

A brief explanation of the medical facts of life, the book's strength is that it reflects different backgrounds (including foster, single parent, familial and other relationships). As it is written from a woman's perspective, the role of the father is seen only occasionally.

The line drawings are, on the whole, clear and support the simple text.

Age: 4 – 6.

ELLIOTT, Michele.
The Willow St Kids — it's your right to be safe.
See CHILD SEXUAL ABUSE

FAGERSTROM, G.
Our New Baby.
Macdonald, (O/P).

Designed to answer young children's questions about the impending birth of a brother or sister, this colourful cartoon-strip picturebook shows what happens when the Williamson family are expecting a new addition. It explains conception, the length of time for foetus development and birth. It also usefully deals with sibling fears and feelings and presents a good atmosphere for questions to be asked and answered.

The book, although designed for young children, uses medical words such as ejaculation and penis, which are adequately explained. The family in question is a white nuclear one, but they live in a block of flats with people of different backgrounds and cultures, so this title could be widely used in many situations.

Age: 3 – 6.

HESSELL, Jenny.
What's wrong with bottoms.
See CHILD SEXUAL ABUSE.

JESSEL, Camilla.
The Joy of Birth.
Methuen, 1982, 0 416 01572 7.

Extremely high quality black and white illustrations are used to good effect to portray the joy and happiness resulting from the birth of a baby. We are taken very quickly through the nine months of pregnancy and onto the birth itself where detailed, close-range photographs show, in context, the baby's entry into the world. The text is brief yet comprehensive and describes the photographs well, so it is not geared to a particular age-range, but, as the subtitle of the paperback edition indicates, it is 'a book for families to share'. The 'family' situation shown is mostly white and nuclear, with photographs of only one black family included. The glossary is very good and detailed, and the book's uses will be very wide in both public libraries (where it could usefully be located in Parent's Collections, as well as children's libraries and integrated stocks) and in school libraries, where it can support the work of many departments.

Age: 5 + .

KITZINGER, Sheila.
Being Born.
Dorling Kindersley, 1986, 0 86318 169 4.

The main focus of the book is the development of the foetus, shown through the superb colour micro-photography of Lennart Nilsson. However, the over-use of such photographic techniques results in too much stress on one part of the body, thus losing the context of birth itself. It is more medical in approach than other items, such as Jessel.

Age: 5 – 16.

LENNET, Robin and CRANE, Bob.
It's OK to say No!: A parent/child manual for the protection of children.
See CHILD SEXUAL ABUSE.

LIFE BEFORE BIRTH.
Pictorial Charts Educational Trust, T45.

Using the micro-photography of Lennart Nilsson, this A2 size chart looks at all stages of physical development, supported by a short accurate text. An information sheet is appended, together with a glossary and a list of suggested questions for group/class work.

Age: 8 – 12.

MAYLE, Peter.
Where did I come from?.
Sun, 1973, 0 7251 0200 4.

An amusing account with cartoon-style illustrations of love-making, conception, pregnancy and birth. While being jocular, it still uses the correct medical words in favour of slang, and conveys the point that love-making and conception are fun and part of a caring relationship. As well as the child's perspective, it includes the adults' experience of lovemaking and pregnancy as warm and loving feelings.

It may partly owe its popularity to the fact that it is a welcome change from many other texts, in that it does not romanticise the subject and injects humour into the text.

Age: 7 – 15.

RAYNER, Claire.
The Body Book.
Andre Deutsch, 1978, 0 233 96989 6.

In simple but accurate language and with clear and sensitive illustrations, this book looks at the total body and its constituent parts. As such, the development of the sex organs and conception is seen in context. The information given is not just medical, for relationships are also covered. It also provides for good body image for both girls and boys, as well as maintaining a multi-cultural context throughout.

Whilst it is a book which younger children can read for themselves, the foreword makes clear the parents role of supporting and providing further information for their children's enquiries, as well as an atmosphere in which a child will feel confident to enquire upon this subject.

Age: 4 – 8.

SHEFFIELD, Margaret.
Where do babies come from?
Cape, 1984 (2nd edition), 0 224 02967 3.

This briefly covers the stages of conception, pregnancy and birth in a factually medical manner, yet the illustrations indicate a magical, beauteous quality, and, as such, over-romanticise the situation.

Age: 5 – 7.

TERKEL, Susan N. and RENCH, Janice E.
Feeling Safe, Feeling Strong.
See CHILD SEXUAL ABUSE.

VEVERS, Gwynne.
Reproduction.
Bodley Head, 1984, 0 370 30992 8.

Quite a lot of information is packed into 24 small pages. Each page is divided between text and illustrations — sometimes a page can be very busy indeed with drawings of people with speech balloons. As such, this is a popular-style presentation, which aids browsing, and is child-centred rather than medical. Nevertheless, body development, conception and birth are adequately covered with proper words used and explained. The illustrations do, happily, indicate a multi-cultural society.

Age: 8 – 11.

WACHTER, Oralee.
No more secrets for me.
See CHILD SEXUAL ABUSE.

WARD, Brian.
Birth and growth.
Franklin Watts, 1983, (O/P).

A mainly comprehensive coverage of these stages of life. Body changes and functions, fertilisation, genes, placenta, foetus growth, birth and twins are all covered in well laid-out double-page spreads where the text, in clear, well-spaced type allows highlighting for medical terms (which are explained in the glossary). Illustrations are also relevant and clear. Nevertheless, the text is slightly coy on conception itself and the information is not presented very clearly.

Age: 9 – 13.

PUBERTY AND ADOLESCENCE

Puberty and Adolescence

Puberty is the age at which young people are most usually deemed to begin to need sexual knowledge; it marks a break with the childhood world of asexual innocence, and there are clear needs — especially about preparing girls for menstruation — which have meant that a lot of sex education has been aimed at young people at this stage of development.

SEX EDUCATION NEEDS AND APPROACHES

Sex education is often included in general biology books and titles about the human body, many produced for schools; and these have only been included in this list where they make a useful contribution to the topic. The great difficulty with these is that sex and reproduction are covered as matters of the body alone, as a series of biological events. However the young adolescent needs to know more than biological information. The sex education needs of this age group include:

1. Learning about the bodily changes of puberty — growth, the development of secondary sexual characteristics, breasts, facial hair, changes in the genitals, menstruation, nocturnal emissions. While these are basically biological phenomena, the reader needs points of identification to relate the material to what is happening to him or her personally, and, above all, to their experience of these changes.

2. Learning about the sexual feelings and sensations which develop in early adolescence. This is a difficult area, but a crucial test of the quality of the sex education is whether it acknowledges the sexuality of adolescents, or whether it attempts to ignore it.

3. Finding information about the sexual world of adults, to counter and balance the 'misinformation' which becomes a matter of currency within peer groups at this age. This means that titles should include a broad range of information, especially that which explains terms which young people may come across — some of which adults would rather keep away from young people.

SELECTION CRITERIA

Approach
Puberty should not be dealt with merely as a matter of biology. The biological changes should be related to practical information about the human body, not just its internal functions: they should be related to the developing awareness of sexuality at adolescence, and the beginnings of ideas of sex in the context of human relationships.

Framework
The starting point for these materials should be the immediate experience of change in the human adolescent body, not the ultimate reproductive purpose of these changes (though this should be mentioned).

An overly reproductive framework has several damaging consequences: it leads to a focus on the internal organs, not external bodily changes; it marginalises the developing sexuality of the reader, and denies her or him the immediate knowledge about new feelings and emotions; and it can imply an exaggerated degree of sexual difference, with boys' bodies being about sex and sexual expression, girls' about having babies. It is also exclusively heterosexual.

Content
* Books should not give an overabundance of unnecessary biological and medical detail on the growth and development of the body, which clouds or obscures the basic information needed.
* Menstruation should not be treated as just a matter of hormones, ovaries and the uterus, but as a new experience around which attitudes to the female body will be formed. *Have you started yet?* is an excellent example.
* Male erections, nocturnal emissions etc should similarly not merely be depicted as a matter of bodily hydraulics — an excess of sperm which must be released.
* Puberty should be marked as the potential beginning of sexual sensations and emotions in both boys and girls. The sexual, as well as the reproductive, organs of girls (including the clitoris) should be described and their function explained.
* Practical information should be given on how to respond to the bodily changes of puberty, and associated health issues (though medical questions should not dominate the texts).
* Texts should encourage positive attitudes to the body and its development.
* Texts should emphasise the range of normal development, and should help young people understand difference — in rates of development, in bodily shapes and sizes, including sexual characteristics.
* Texts should give an awareness of differences in attitudes to the body, to nudity, menstruation, emission of sperm etc, in the context of family and religious attitudes to sexual development.

Style and vocabulary
* Many of the titles for this age group are designed to be read directly by young people, so the style needs to be accessible and readable. While the 'correct'

vocabulary should be used, the tone should not be too objectively neutral — the reader needs points of identification.

* Collections should include some child-centred texts, such as *The Body Book*, Meredith's *Facts of Life*, Mayle's *What's happening to me*, which are popular/irreverent in tone.

* Texts should give information about sexual terms and concepts which young adolescents will hear about in the media, peer group etc, and explain them.

* Glossaries and indexes are particularly important in this context, and should give alternative terms (slang and scientific).

Illustrations
Many of these present difficulties for selectors because of their lavish illustrations of the human body. This can be useful in illustrating the range of 'normal' development, but an overglossy presentation may be a point of embarrassment for young people as well as adults, particularly where used in a group context.

At the other extreme, the illustrative style should not glamourise the human body through the use of soft focus photography or of idealised physical types.

Texts should show physical development and growth through a careful range of images of the body, not just through diagrams which divorce the internal organs from the whole.

BALDWIN, Dorothy and LISTER, C.
How you grow and change.
Wayland, 1983, 0 85078 333 X.

This text begins and ends with reproduction, and where the changes of puberty are secondary to the life cycle, ie. becoming a parent.

Altogether, rather a cosy, white, middle-class image is projected especially through the many colour illustrations. The psychological aspects of puberty are skated over and there is little intimation that sexual intercourse and conception can be a pleasurable and beautiful experience. The overall impression is clinical and cold.

Nevertheless, the text is well-written with medical terms properly used and explained, and is supplemented by a glossary. The standard of production is high, and print size, illustrations and photographs supplement the text well.

BIRKE, L. and GARDNER, K.
Why suffer?: Periods and their problems.
Virago, 1982 (2nd edition), 0 86068 284 6.

Aimed at an adult audience, this title looks in depth at the menstrual cycle. In particular, it deals with the causes of pre-menstrual tension and offers advice on dealing with this (the second edition incorporates feedback from readers of the first edition, which appears in the section on PMT) and the book also discusses irregular periods. The book includes medical information and looks positively at the female body — as such, it could be said to follow on from Thomson (see later in this section) and provide further reading for older teenage girls.

An annotated book list and a glossary appear at the end of the book.

DAY, Roger and C.
Help! I'm growing up: a child/parent guide to sex and puberty.
Harvestime, 1987, 0 947714 18 9.

Aimed at both parents and young people, this is a strictly Christian approach, in which adolescents are told everything they are deemed to need to know about sex until they marry. It advocates that a young person reads it with a parent — "Dad if you're a boy, Mum if you're a girl" — and discusses it. Likewise it advises parents not to avoid the issue and leave this subject to anyone else. Sexual relations are only deemed permissible between married partners and are for procreational reasons, although the enjoyment of sex is seen as a gift of God. The book covers emotional aspects as well as medical information, all of which are based on biblical teaching, with many references to the Bible to be followed up.

There are chapters for boys or girls only to read and these contain information on their own bodies, sex organs, etc., which is not regarded as necessary information for the other sex. It is also difficult for a girl to get a positive view of her own body from this book.

AIDS (which is seen as a punishment) and sexual abuse are included, as is homosexuality. One reason for the latter existing is that 'when a nation becomes increasingly evil, more of its people deliberately choose to turn to homosexuality.' Thus, gay people are stereotyped and judged to be guilty of sin.

Much attention is given to upholding Christian values in adolescence and unhelpful advice is given, including 'Boys, be real young men. Girls, become lovely young ladies.' It also gives advice on being 'unequally yoked' ie. "...it is wrong for a Christian to marry a non-Christian" and "...this applies...to going out together."

The text is brief, broken up by many sub-headings and is written alternately in the first and third person. In places, the text reads patronisingly and is not aided by the indiscriminate use of the exclamation mark. Throughout the book, there are spaces for the reader to fill in the answer, having looked up the reference in the Bible, and a list of questions about sex, again to be filled in, is appended, which will in itself make the book unsuitable for lending library use.

DOAN, Helen and MORSE, J.
Every girl.
Stoddart, 1985, 0 7737 5027 4

Designed as a handbook for 'young girls and the caring adults' this provides basic and well-explained information and practical advice on menstruation. It seeks to answer common questions and worries and this is done briefly and adequately.

The authors surveyed a range of girls in Canada and their responses are incorporated in the book; as such, it involves girls' own experiences and perceptions. Unfortunately it does not succeed in going further, to provide adequate analysis of the views of those surveyed. It certainly does not help improve a girl's self-image of her body, and although touching on the mystique of menstruation in contemporary society, does not provide strategies for improving the situation eg. being frank with boys. Indeed, by describing itself as a handbook for young girls only, it denies boys the opportunity of acquiring information and understanding of this development.

The book concludes with a mostly unnecessary chapter of irrelevant information on menstruation, which most unfortunately includes a section on 'women in primitive societies'.

While brief and readable, the text is geared to Canadian readership and is uninterestingly laid out on the page, with few illustrations, though with a well-designed cover.

DOCHERTY, James.
Growing up.
Modus, 1986, 0 948881 00 3; 0 948881 01 1.

This book attempts a more explicit approach to the development of the body, and the text, written from a medical perspective, is full and detailed. It covers puberty and reproduction, with a smaller section looking at growing awareness of sexuality, masturbation, menstruation, sexual abuse and hygiene, together with emotional experiences. While responsibility is covered, the more adult aspects of sexual development and orientation, and contraception, are not included (these are intended to be covered in a companion volume).

Published in association with the Royal Society of Medicine, it uses medical terms rather than common names or slang terms and these are extended by a comprehensive glossary. A full index allows immediate access to specific information and a useful book list for further reading is appended.

The text is liberally illustrated with colour photographs (and includes images of black as well as white bodies), the intention of which is to make perfectly clear what the text explains. The photographs do indeed fulfil this objective, but it has been seen in practice, that the explicit photographs prevent adults from using it with their children and that pupils may not use the book in a structured way.

GROWING UP.
4 wallcharts + notes.
Pictorial Chart Educational Trust, 1988, T741.

The posters cover puberty, body changes of both males and females, and periods.

All are clearly presented, using bright colours, graphics and clear diagrams and cartoons. The chart on periods is particularly well-explained, with a key to the menstrual cycle, though there is little note of periods which do not fit into a 28 day cycle. The notes include a case study of various characters (who appear on the cartoons) at all stages of puberty, and suggests several discussion themes using these characters. This sheet may be reproduced for class use.

GREENWOOD, T. and FENNESSY, S.
I don't want to know: towards a healthy adolescence.
Hutchinson of Australia, 1986, (O/P).

This regards adolescence as a valid point of being, not just a stage to be passed through as quickly as possible. Using the device of fictionalised episodes to illustrate aspects of adolescence — body image, body development, feelings, fears, emotions, relationships, drugs and sex — the authors then seek to explain and understand these concerns. While this is a good idea, it does not go far enough — not only are too few subjects covered but those which are, give only sketchy information and points of view. The reader will be left wondering 'what next'/ 'and'? The book does not suggest any further means of information at all.

The text is not well laid out and the overall impression is boring. Moreover, it was first published in Australia, and includes some slang words not understandable in the United Kingdom and more importantly, does not cater for differing societal structure with which a British reader will be familiar.

HAMPTON, J.
Healthy living, healthy loving: a guide to happy, healthy relationships and family life.
Macmillan, 1987, (O/P).

Brief but adequate coverage is given to physical and emotional aspects of puberty. Relationships covered include polygamy, child marriage and the extended family but the main thrust is on relationships within marriage and sex for procreational reasons.

The introduction refers to programmes of population education in some African countries, and this is reflected in the fact that much attention is given to pregnancy, birth, child spacing and contraception. Thus the book would appear to be published initially for use in health education programmes in certain African states.

Sexual intercourse is, of course, covered, as is sexually transmitted diseases, including AIDS, where useful and practical advice is given. Homosexuality is briefly but well explained and ameliorates stereotyping.

Feelings, caring attitudes and responsibilities for both partners are integral to the text and the use of agony-aunt style letters allows specific and common problems/ aspects to be aired, as well as many myths to be debunked. The text does promote good self image for a female body.

The cover photograph and many illustrations show that this is one of the few texts which cater for a black readership.

HODSON, Philip.
Letters to Growing Pains.
BBC, 1988, 0 563 20635 7.

Covers in a general way many aspects of puberty and human behaviour, and offers brief common-sense advice. Topics covered include family relationships, fears, friendship, skin problems, and periods. Any further sexual information is not given.

The book's strength is that it gives young teenagers the opportunity to air their own concerns and advice is given on a core of similar enquiries.

Although the author, an agony-uncle from children's television, makes reference to useful books in the text, there is no booklist appended, nor an index, so this title is really for the browser. Nevertheless, it will be a reassuring read for younger teenagers concerned with the advent of puberty.

KEABLE-ELLIOTT, D.
You and your body.
Arrow, 1983, (O/P).

This incorporates a wide range of topics — generally, each subject area, ranging from general health, skin problems, to personality and relationships, forms a chapter with information given in alphabetical order of topic or aspects and sub-headings where necessary. As such, it is a good reference tool for young people who can check information privately.

In addition, an extended section provides information on the stages of sexual intercourse.

KINGSTON, Beryl.
Lifting the curse: how to relieve painful periods.
Sheldon Press, 1980, 0 85969 408 9.

This provides medical explanation, reassurance and practical help where period pain is severe. As such it is aimed at all women, but includes a section on how to cope at school. Not only is practical daily advice given but strategies to ease the situation, ranging from seeking help/understanding from staff to pressing for a change of policy at school to make things easier (eg. to wear trousers or stay indoors at break). Diagrams help illustrate points but the print-size is very small which makes reading difficult. Nevertheless, this is still a most useful item for specific needs.

A LOOK AT YOUR BODY (poster).
Brook Advisory Centres.

A large two-colour poster showing the male and female sex organs, with the medical or correct names clearly labelled. In spite of its size (57 x 76 cms) it cannot usefully be viewed from afar as there is a good deal of detail given on the poster.

MacFARLANE, Aidan and McPHERSON, A.
The Diary of a Teenage Health Freak.
OUP, 1987, 0 19 286083 6.
"On re-reading the book I was struck by the amount of down-to-earth frankness about sex. My neurosis about this subject, especially about the length of my 'thing' has now diminished. Here are all the answers to the questions I've never dared to ask." (Adrian Mole: foreword).

The format and style owes its origins to the hugely popular diaries of Adrian Mole. Peter Payne is almost the same age as Adrian (14 years and 1 month as opposed to 13¾!) and we have here an amusing account of both Peter and his family's preoccupations, worries, fears, etc. about growing up and becoming sexually aware. Although written in diary form, each chapter takes a topic or theme, such as periods, 'life change', STD and so on. Nevertheless, some information may only be covered briefly or perhaps not at all, but an index helps.

This is an amusing approach, it has proved a popular format with young people from 11 to 16 and may be viewed as supporting material — it will certainly issue well from a teenage collection.

MEREDITH, Susan.
Facts of life.
Usborne, 1985, 0 86020 869 9.
(Also published separately as *Growing Up* and *Babies*).

An amalgam of *Growing Up* and *Babies*, this presents a wide range of information in the well-known Usborne house style, utilizing a bright range of print, graphics and sketches to supplement the text. It is popular and chatty in tone and child-centred in approach.

The text is short, but contains essential biological information, whether on body changes, puberty, menstruation or sexual intercourse. Occasionally, the short items of information can be simplistic, but this occurs infrequently. The biological information is the best presented — the emotional aspects and responsibility, while mentioned, are not made much of.

A good glossary is appended, as is a booklist and the authors have as special consultants a gynaecologist and the Marriage Guidance Council.

MILLER, Jonathan and PELHAM, D.
The Facts of Life: a three-dimensional study.
Cape, 1984, 0 224 02242 3.

The information given is entirely biologically-based; each page of this 'pop-up' book is devoted to detailed 3-D illustrations of sexual organs with the exception of the first and last pages, which show the foetus at different stages of development.

Pages are literally crammed with information and illustration, so much so that it is difficult to understand what is being presented. While undoubtedly a feat of paper technology, its usefulness in giving relevant information in an accessible manner to young people is limited, although it could effectively be used in a highly-structured way with very small groups of students.

PICKERING, Lucienne.
Boys talk; Girls talk.
Cassell, 1981, 0 225 66309 0; 0 225 66310 4.

Although no doubt useful when first published, the text now reads in a coy and sometimes patronising and moralistic tone. The author assumes a middle-class, stereotyped family as the norm and everything is related to that.

The device of using an extract with fictional characters to start, and then giving information on the topic in question, works better for some aspects than others. If anything, *Girls talk* is the less useful, as everything seems geared towards pregnancy and birth.

The production is uninteresting with idealised line-drawings; no useful information is appended, nor is there an index.

(See also *Parents listen* in the section 'Material for parents, carers and teachers').

SPROULE, Anna.
Whose body is it?.
Macdonald, 1987, 0 356 13410 5.

In a wide-ranging coverage of many issues connected with the human body, the author includes abortion, sexuality, sex education, contraception and AIDS. Each topic is covered in a two-page spread, where the text is varied with photographs, captions, media reports, etc., in the *Debates* series style.

The text features various issues or questions concerned with a topic and briefly but succinctly answers these. Indeed, the topic headings appear as questions, eg. Keeping it in the family? (sex education) and The aim of love? (contraception). While this can be accused of simplicity, it presents topics in a debatable and accessible form. The book concerns itself with people of various cultures, religions and sexual orientation, and provides points of experience for the reader to evaluate his/her view of their own body.

The excellent reading list comprises book titles, reports, journals and newspaper articles, as well as a list of useful addresses.

THOMSON, Ruth.
Have you started yet?
Piccolo, 1980, 0 330 26134 7.

A helpful book for teenagers on menstruation. The author used questionnaires and interviews as a starting point for the book, and deals with questions and concerns reflecting the responses of those interviewed.

Periods are not defined as a 'problem' but seen in the context of a range of experiences and responses, so the book is more than just medical in content. It does not focus on the reproductive system, but is positive about the way girls should see the female body and its changes. The concise text provides practical information and advice and helps break the mystique and secrecy surrounding periods. A small section called 'Boys and periods' points out that girls should not keep this perfectly natural development a secret from boys.

A glossary and limited book list are appended, together with a comprehensive index.

TEENAGE SEXUAL AWARENESS AND ACTIVITY

Teenage Sexual Awareness and Activity

It is at this level that selection becomes fraught with difficulties, since we encounter the debates about sexual morality, homosexuality, AIDS etc. These debates, and the problem of developing a professional response, were discussed in the general introduction to this guide. However in selecting texts for the teenage years it is vital that we consider them in relation to a range of criteria, not just on the treatment of 'difficult' topics.

SEX EDUCATION NEEDS AND APPROACHES

Books for the adolescent and teenage years tend to be written from either a medical or a human relations perspective, though all combine some elements of both.

1. Health education: the medical perspective

These are written primarily from a medical perspective, and deal essentially with the biology of sex. Health education can, in many cases, be criticised for being overly focussed on the biology of sex and reproduction, and care should be taken to look at how well the medical perspectives are linked to developing ideas about human relationships, emotions, and needs.

Health education approaches might seem as if they belong purely to the realm of science, but in fact all embody strong sets of values and attitudes. Morality is included along with the science (e.g. the idea of the family as the only natural form of social arrangement; of homosexuality as a disease of the mind or body) even where human relationships are not discussed explicitly.

AIDS is a crucial dimension of health education, and many texts are now being produced around this topic. These are discussed in a separate section; but note that general titles should be assessed on the coverage and treatment of this topic.

2. Education in personal relations

Dealing with the education of the whole person, not just with the biology of sex, these titles are broader in their educational approach. The best provide biological knowledge along with materials to help young people think through and develop their own values and attitudes, using discussion techniques, case studies, etc. The

32

overriding concept is the development of personal responsibility in human relationships, from a background of understanding the emotional and psychological, as well as the physical, basis of relationships.

This category includes texts with a strong educational line (e.g. Wellings) and texts written from a teenage perspective on issues arising in human and sexual relationships (e.g. Stoppard, Haywood).

SELECTION CRITERIA
The criteria for selecting titles for this age group should be based on the comments at the beginning of the section on puberty and adolescence, in terms of style, vocabulary, illustrations etc. In addition the following criteria need to be considered.

Moral framework
* Texts should not separate the biology of sex from the context of human relationships.
* Texts should present sexuality in a moral framework which acknowledges the importance of the social context of human relationships and the family. However they should not avoid discussion of sexuality and sexual relationships during the teenage years.
* We need to provide materials which reflect the views of different religions and groups. Texts should acknowledge the variations in what is defined as 'moral' in different religions and cultures.

Style and approach
* The texts need to stress the importance of the human relations dimension of sexuality without over-romanticising it, either through the text itself or the illustrations.
* The texts need to acknowledge the diversity of patterns of relationships and family forms; and to reflect different class and ethnic backgrounds.
* The approach of many texts is to encourage the development of personal morality in decision making, and responsibility in relationships: this means a particular educational strategy which provides young people with a framework for developing their values and attitudes. Discussion material, case studies, personal accounts etc. are useful techniques (as in Saunders, and the strategies outlined in *Taught not caught*).
* Texts are required at different levels and for different audiences and we should include those which reflect the experiences of young people themselves.

Practical relevance
* Practical information is required as well as discussion (especially on contraception, AIDS, teenage pregnancy); and this needs to be easily accessible, rather than wrapped up in too much discussion. Chapter headings and indexes, glossaries and so on are good indications.
* Texts should include information and advice on sources of help and information to young people. This should be up to date and practical.

Treatment of homosexuality

Texts should not present homosexuality as an illness or disease. While texts cannot legally 'promote' homosexuality, selectors should consider the implications of reading the text for a young person who may consider her/himself to be a lesbian or homosexual.

ADAMS, Carol and LAURIKIETIS, R.
The Gender Trap: a closer look at sex roles — 2: Sex and marriage.
Virago, 1980 (2nd edition), 0 704 33802 5.

Aimed at young people, this looks at sex stereotyping and examines many attitudes, pressures and expectations in the area of sex and marriage.

Double standards for females and males are examined in such aspects as dating, contraception, bodies, social conventions and sex appeal. Lesbianism and homosexuality, rape, battered wives, one-parent families and the glamourisation of motherhood are also covered.

In a lively text, which is enhanced by judicious use of poetry, stories/extracts and quotes, the authors ask questions of the reader and provide points of focus to consider. It provides a useful survey and background information on the pressures which condition male/female attitudes and relationships, and offers a feminist viewpoint. A useful bibliography (including a comprehensive film section) is appended.

BELL, Ruth and others.
Changing Bodies, Changing Lives: a book for teens on sex and relationships.
Random House, 1987 (2nd edition), 0 394 56499 5.

The authors include members of the Boston Women's Health Book Collective as well as teenagers. Indeed the book allows teenagers to speak themselves through its many quotes from young people's experiences and perspectives. A main tenet of the book is that accurate information on all aspects of development is essential and this the book provides — as well as medical information, the relationship/ emotional aspects are fully covered. The book promotes good feelings about one's body for both sexes and points out responsibility and decision-making rests with both partners. Its coverage of homosexuality is comprehensive, it debunks myths and occurs logically in the book rather than an appendix. The book has been updated to provide information of AIDS, which is helpful and not written in an atmosphere of panic.

The text is easy to read yet provides enough detail on each aspect, although this is entirely US-based as is its grammar, so this can be a drawback. The layout is full, with little variation in size and use of graphics, nor are the illustrations of good quality, though they do show a multi-cultural society.

BENEDICT, Helen.
Safe, Strong and Streetwise — the teenage survival guide.
See CHILD SEXUAL ABUSE.

34

BOYS, Philip and PEARLMAN, C. (editors).
The Comic Book of First Love.
Virago, 1988, 0 86068 187 4.

A light-hearted yet pertinent look at situations, pressures and expectations which may face many teenagers embarking upon amatory experiences — or not, as the case may be. Over a dozen contributors provide, in a comic-book format, wry humour and irony in looking at different occasions encountered by both sexes. Some of the humour is very sophisticated and may demand a more mature reader but nevertheless the book manages to inject new ideas and different approaches which could be used constructively in particular circumstances by teachers or librarians, or indeed for purely browsing purposes. This is part of the Virago *Upstarts* series and as such its size follows the house style which is at the expense of some pages being very packed and dense, where a larger size would have been preferable.

BOYS TALKING.
cassette + notes, 7CK/353, 1980;
GIRLS TALKING ABOUT SEX EDUCATION.
cassette + notes, 13CK/154, 1980.
Brook Advisory Centres.

Both tapes include young people talking about aspects of sex education. However, both are quite different and so their uses are various.

Boys talking is divided into four parts. Boys were interviewed about their feelings about sex and encouraged to talk about relationships with girls, sexual activity, responsibility and contraception. At first, the interviewer adopts a mainly directed or closed-end questioning approach, but this is soon diffused, allowing the tape and its accompanying notes to be used to promote discussion.

Girls talking about sex education is more comprehensive: part I features teenage girls with a wide range of sexual experiences who talk frankly, including how they found out about 'the birds and the bees' (as one girl put it), whether from family, playground, teachers, friends, other agencies or none of these. The other aim of this tape is to encourage discussion among parents, teachers and other concerned groups about their responsibilities and participation — this is admirably done, and the cassette concludes that this is not a special compartment but an aspect of everyday life which should be covered naturally and certainly where information should be available when and where it is needed.

BROWN, Fern G.
Childbirth.
Franklin Watts, 1989, 0 86313 791 1.

Extremely practical and reassuring, this title is devoted to the actual birth of a child. The options open to parents are described and the reader follows three couples as they face the delivery of their child — one needing a caesarian delivery, one a more conventional delivery (but done in a squatting position and requiring an episiotomy) and the third, a natural birth at home. The delivery of the placenta is described as well as after-birth stages, including bonding.

Clear, accurate photographs aid a brief, comprehensive and informal text, and one in which medical terms are well explained (there is also a glossary).

This really does cover well a baby's birth and throughout includes the father as well as the mother in as many stages as possible. Its uses will be many, including the young parent, childcare courses, sex education and PSE programmes in school.

COUSIN-MILLS, Jane.
Make it Happy, Make it Safe: what sex is all about.
Penguin, 1988, 0 14 010713 4.

Originally written in 1978, the author took the point of view that sex is a "healthy and natural part of our lives". As such, a commonsense approach was taken in a book which was comprehensive, clear and practical without being wordy and simplistic. This has not changed in the 1988 publication, which is essentially re-written, rather than being a revision of a previous edition. The title too has changed, with the phrase 'make it safe' being added, thus echoing present climate — nevertheless, within this framework, the accent is on 'happy'.

Body changes, especially of the sex organs, are well explained, using medical terms with their colloquial names. Emotional aspects are included, as is the role which society expects both females and males to play. The book promotes positive attitudes towards self and developing sexuality, and is not biological in viewpoint — this is one of the few titles which carries this for girls.

Masturbation and orgasms are covered in detail, as are sexual practices. The author gives full information on such matters but takes a realistic line and makes the point that one should not be coerced into sexual practices.

Contraception receives comprehensive coverage and addresses the subject of responsibility whilst exploding various myths associated with types of birth control. In particular, the advantages and disadvantages (including long-term ones) of the Pill are pointed out. Pregnancy and abortion receive similar treatment and the book concludes with a useful section on the laws relating to sex and young people and a brief coverage of health care, including a growing awareness of cancer, as well as sexually transmitted diseases (STD). In addition to information on venereal disease, the book provides essential information on AIDS. An extremely comprehensive list of addresses of relevant organisations, a booklist and an excellent index complete this title which is deservedly popular and has won awards.

GREENWOOD, Judy.
Personal relationships.
Chambers, 1986, 0 550 20566 7.

This deals with a wide range of relationships, including those in the community, family and friends. It advises on care and consideration for other people as well as ensuring 'space' for the reader. The author looks at stereotyping and blurred or changing roles in today's society, eg. fatherhood. Body language and self-esteem are considered important and while Greenwood is at pains to point out that everyone is individual, nevertheless uses the term 'normal' as a yardstick. Lastly, sexual relationships are covered and the author advocates care, thought and responsibility by both partners and gives a list of where to seek further advice, before finally offering some advice on marriage.

The text is easy to read and well broken-up, with good print size, though inferior line-drawings.

GUNN, A.
Sex and You: an illustrated guide to the facts of life for young people.
Macdonald, 1986, (O/P).

A well-produced and comprehensive book, dealing with mostly the biological aspects of sexual development: body changes, including breast and genital growth, relationships, sexual intercourse and sexual difficulties. Problems of health are briefly dealt with in an alphabetical sequence, including AIDS.

A detailed section on conception, contraception, pregnancy and abortion appears; sexual abuse and legal points also receive coverage.

All topics are accompanied by helpful charts, diagrams and both colour and black and white illustrations, which assist a very readable text. It is good to see the sexual needs of disabled people covered in the main body of the book and not as a separate chapter or appendix.

However, the title is dominated by bodily changes and physical factors and does not cover adequately the aspects of relationships and emotions.

HART, John.
So you think you're attracted to the same sex?
Penguin, 1984, 0 14 006715 9.

This social study of homosexuality is aimed at an adult or older teenage audience. Its scope is wide-ranging and its vocabulary level high. Looking at sexual, political and social aspects, it examines discrimination against homosexuals and lesbians. The author writes from his own experience, but also uses case studies and academic research.

It covers sexuality, identity and lifestyle while other sections include bisexuality and a look at the causes of homosexuality (both from a parent's and a child's point of view). An interesting study of politics and sexuality (mostly of the 1970's and early '80's), lists the Gay Charter and covers the emotional/psychological aspects of same-sex relationships and advice on 'coming out'.

The book explains and answers the need for information, and is positive in that it demistifies stereotypes but it does not promote homosexuality. However the nature of the title — it is an adult and not an adolescent perspective — makes it more suitable for older age groups (18 +).

HAYMAN, Susie.
It's more than just sex!: a survival guide to the teenage years.
Wildwood House, 1986, 0 7045 0512 6.

While the author indeed covers many aspects of interest to teenagers, just under half of this book comes under the scope of this booklist as it includes information on puberty, periods and wet dreams, erections, pregnancy, STD, abortion, contraception and homosexuality.

The wide range of contents provides good practical information and options and is not only medically-based, so it deals with problems and issues in teenage sexuality and relationships in a positive and helpful way.

In its coverage of homosexuality, it explores stereotypes but makes the law and society's rules clear, and provides information on how to cope if the reader thinks s/he is gay.

While written in a straightforward way, the chapters/sections would be improved if divided by sub-headings but the index allows swift location of specific information. Line drawings break up and supplement the text of this 'street-wise' title and a useful list of addresses of relevant organisations is appended.

HEALTHDATA.
Healthdata
Dr C Dobbling
21 Vicars Close, London E9 7HT, 01-985 3043.

This provides information (of GCSE level and approach) of a medical nature and common-sense advice on a wide range of health issues, including contraception, AIDS, STD, pregnancy and period pains.

The information, on viewdata page format, is, of necessity, brief and to the point but is relevant and up-to-date. Other material will be needed to provide more details and to stimulate thought but, nevertheless, this approach may be useful for many students, it can be used as part of a formal education programme or, access permitting, as a means of private enquiry.

As well as an online facility, the most important information is now available on disc for BBC and Nimbus micro-computers.

HEMMING, J.
Teenage Living and Loving. 0 7279 0017 X.
TRIMMER, E.
Knowing about Sex. 0 7279 0110 9.
Family Doctor Publications/BMA, 1986.

Teenage Living and Loving is a brief guide which concentrates on the emotional development of teenagers. In accessible, though slightly formal language, the author looks at the self-discovery which teenagers face in the years of maturity. The reader is asked to think about responsibility for his/her actions. The author assumes heterosexual relationships to be the norm.

Knowing about Sex provides answers to many questions asked of a practicing doctor, including detailed aspects of sexual intercourse. The author takes as a basic tenet that information is useful — 'giving the facts leads only to giving people the chance to make good judgement and opt for sensible choices.'

However a major drawback must be that the medical perspective is separated from the social and relationship aspects in these two books, thus making them individually of little value. Furthermore, they are poorly produced: for example, the text appears cramped on the page and there is no index.

JARVIS, Debra.
Take it again from the Top — life and love, fat and fitness.
Lion, 1986, 0 7459 1138 2.

The author reviews her own puberty, family pressures and relationships and presents a Christian viewpoint. As a marathon runner, she uses the analogy with spiritual fitness. A 'checkout' list of options, myths and ideas are appended to the end of each section for the reader to consider. The book's strength is that it makes demands of the reader by asking her/him to assess the situation and think it through, and, in an easy to read and not dogmatic text, gives the account of one person's experience.

KELLY, Gary.
Learning about Sex: the contemporary guide for young adults.
Barron, 1987, 0 8120 2432 X.

The author (a counsellor and sex therapist) makes his own values clear at the start: he thinks sex is a beautiful thing but one must take responsibility for one's own actions — and the readers must decide for themselves.

He asks the reader to take space and answer questions about him/herself, while answering the questions many young people would like answered.

As this is a US publication, much information is slanted towards an American audience — the statistics are all American, as are the titles he recommends for further reading at the end of each chapter. Another reservation is that the illustrations are infrequent and of poor quality, and a major problem is the exclusion of information on AIDS.

LAWSON, Michael and SKIPP, D.
Sex and That: what's it all about?
Lion, 1985, 0 85648 782 1.

This provides basic medical information and further discussion of the emotional side of growing up. Such information and practice is continually measured against Biblical teaching and Christian values. This is made quite clear, for example, in discussing sex before marriage, abortion and homosexuality. Throughout, a heterosexual relationship is the only form countenanced, and one where young people measure themselves against 'normal' criteria. The authors' view of homosexuality is that it is an adolescent stage which will soon be passed over. Where adults have a homosexual relationship, that is a disease for which the adults are not responsible and they deserve compassion and forgiveness. Other information in the book is also unreliable, eg. contraception, which is extremely simplistic.

The illustrations, mostly cartoon-style, are poor and dated, the poem which ends the book 'Sex is like a gift wrapped in brown paper' is extremely twee, and there is no index.

LLEWELLYN-JONES, Derek.
Everygirl.
OUP (Australia), 1987, 0 19 554710 1.

Although covering all the experiences and emotions of a teenage girl, this book concentrates on many topics concerned with sex education. Indeed, its coverage is most comprehensive, giving as it does information on reproduction, menstruation, sexual behaviour, pregnancy, contraception, abortion and sexual assault.

While taking a morally neutral tone, the text explains the options/choices available, explodes popular myths and deals with associated emotional areas of growing sexual awareness. Topics are often covered in an historical context and they lead on to advocate positive female gender roles and values. However, while lesbianism is briefly covered, heterosexual relationships are assumed to be the norm.

The text, although detailed, is well laid-out but is biased to Australian practice, as it was first published in that country, so some medical practice/structure and, for example, contraceptive products may be different to this country. A few photographs do not marry well with the text and on two pages, the reader is invited to fill in a chart and to annotate a drawing of female genital organs, which may mitigate against effective lending library use.

LLEWELLYN-JONES, Derek.
Understanding Sexuality.
OUP (Australia), 1989 (3rd edition), 0 19 554928 7.

This begins with puberty and deals with a range of issues, both physical and emotional, and concludes this section by saying "sex is...communicating your thoughts and feelings to your loved one" — an aspect often ignored in relationships.

Topics include family planning, abortion, pregnancy, infertility, STD (although there is little on AIDS, it is otherwise comprehensive) and 'alternative' sexual lifestyles, ending with rape and the answering of common problems.

The text throughout is balanced and reasonable and is liberally and well illustrated. However the text shows it was first published in Australia and refers to agencies and laws there. The book may be used for group work as it gives practical points and activity suggestions at the end of each chapter, such as highlighting particular issues to be investigated and listing questions to be discussed.

McCORMACK, Andrina and McCALL SMITH, E.
All about Sex.
Chambers, 1987, 0 550 20570 5.

This gives clear information on emotional and physical aspects of sex and growing sexual awareness. Its scope encompasses periods, erections, masturbation, love and intercourse, and gives detailed information on contraception, although it is too simplistic when it states the Pill has few side effects. While it discusses bisexuality and homosexuality briefly, a heterosexual relationship is assumed throughout. The book emphasises the importance of responsibility in relationships. The authors use a chatty tone, but also somewhat odd language at times, eg. 'little boys and little girls' and 'boys and how they work', which is patronising and sexist. While the brief text is fairly well laid out, the overall production is poor, with few illustrations and no index.

NOURSE, Alan E.
Birth Control.
Franklin Watts, 1989, 0 86313 789 X.

Written in a chatty, straight-forward manner, this concise title looks at the reasons for birth control and the variety of methods which may be employed. This encompasses brief but comprehensive coverage of natural methods of birth control and 'artificial' or barrier methods. More detail is devoted to the Pill but earlier methods and not fully recommended methods, such as the mini-Pill, are also included.

The author also points out that sex can be refused, for various reasons, including religious and moral ones, and that both partners need to be aware of the necessity for birth control and not assume it to be the responsibility of the other partner.

Finally, abortion is covered from a practical viewpoint only (so that, for instance, no mention is made of the Alton-lobby and the moral/religious objection to abortion.)

A very readable text is supported by relevant photographs and diagrams while boxed sections draw attention to specific aspects. A useful glossary is appended but there is no list of further reading nor list of relevant organisations.

NOURSE, Alan E.
Safe sex.
Franklin Watts, 1989, 0 86313 790 3.

The title indicates a strategy to be adopted in relation to the danger of sexually-transmitted diseases. Brief but comprehensive coverage of bacteria and viruses set the medical scene, before proceeding to discuss and explain a variety of STD'S — AIDS, of course, being the most serious, but including genital herpes, syphilis and others. Symptoms are explained, as are the implications, treatment and prevention. Coverage of AIDS is seen in context, so is not written in an atmosphere of panic and fear; the text also stresses that the disease is not a 'gay' one.

The book concludes with advocating safe sex practices, provides practical advice in encouraging each partner to be fully responsible and includes the right to say 'no' or defer having sex until later.

The well-written text, printed in clear type and supported by good, clear graphics and apt photographs with an adequate glossary and index, is easy to read and understand yet still retains medical terms and accuracy. The book succeeds in its aim of presenting relevant information (to young adults) with which they can make responsible decisions.

SAUNDERS, Deborah.
Let's discuss Sex.
Wayland, 1987, 0 85078 916 8.

A useful, well-written discussion of topics relating to sex. It starts by pointing out that people are inculcated with values and morals from childhood and this will have a bearing on sexual relationships. This is extended by looking at how the sexes are viewed in different cultures. As such, this is an innovative approach to the development of personal decision-making and responsibility. It will be a most useful tool in schools, particularly for personal and social education courses.

It is an exemplary mix of both physical and emotional information and points of view, so short chapters, with black and white illustrations, examine topics such as pregnancy, contraception (including male sterilisation — an aspect not often mentioned), infertility, abortion, sex education, society and sexual orientations.

Technique to promote decision-making include suggestions for group discussion at the end of each chapter as well as three case studies (where topics include family discussion of sex and marriage v. living together) which are not subject to copyright and may be reproduced for use in the classroom.

SHARPE, Sue.
Falling for Love: teenage mothers talk.
Virago, 1987, 0 86068 841 0.

When Michelle, a teenager from the BBC series *Eastenders* became pregnant, it struck a chord with many in the same situation. At this time, Sue Sharpe wrote several articles in magazines on the subject and received a great deal of feedback, so she decided to do more research and interviewed around thirty teenagers. These interviews form the basis of this book — teenage girls talking about their problems, their feelings, their aspirations. It is entirely societal in outlook, with chapters on sex and contraception, parents and relationships, education, housing, disability, adoption and abortion. It concludes with a list of helpful addresses.

The text demands good reading skills but it is broken up into regular paragraphs and quotes from teenagers themselves and, as such, is a compelling read.

STEWART, B.
Sex for young people with spina bifida or cerebral palsy.
ASBAH (Association for Spina Bifida and Hydrocephalus), 1983 (2nd edition), 0 906687 03 9.

A well-written book for teenagers giving all the salient points about sex, relationships, body changes, contraception, etc., after which the author looks at the difficulties which spina bifida and cerebral palsy may or may not cause to relationships and sexual intercourse. The problem of a child being born to handicapped parents is also examined and two case studies are included of disabled couples — one contemplating marriage, and the other a married couple with two children. A glossary, list of helpful organisations and reading list are appended but, unfortunately, no index.

STONES, Rosemary.
Loving Encounters: a book for teenagers about sex.
Piccadilly, 1988, 1 85340 005 X.

This looks briefly but comprehensively at all aspects of sex, ranging from purely biological information to practical considerations, and examines feelings and relationships. It draws attention to the development of sexual awareness and looks at different sexual orientations which it explains and discusses rationally and without bias. Indeed, the author rebuffs the labelling of people, eg. straight, gay, etc. and points out that people are complex individuals and cannot easily be compartmentalised. Stones also looks at when teenagers 'should' have sex and concludes that it is for an individual to decide freely. She advises on safeguards and advocates both partners taking responsibility.

The main part of the book discusses safer sex in relation to AIDS. It is quite clear on how one does and does not become HIV infected and looks in detail at different sexual activities in terms of risk factors. Stones advises what to do if you know a partner has AIDS and includes detailed information on contraception methods. The author equally covers the enjoyment of sexual activities and the limits placed on teenagers by the law. This eminently practical book concludes with an excellent list of where to get help and advice.

The text is most readable and explains new phenomena and terms logically and easily. The use of street language terms will not offend its intended reader but may cause reservations in others. The book has been well received, can be used in a variety of situations in schools and would also be a useful addition to teenage sections of public libraries. Likewise, the use of the book in terms of age ranges will depend on local factors — in practice this has varied from 12 to 14/15 years as a lower age band.

STONES, Rosemary.
Too Close Encounters and what to do about them — a guide for teenagers.
See CHILD SEXUAL ABUSE.

STOPPARD, Miriam.
Talking Sex — a book about growing up.
Gollancz, 1982, (O/P); Piccolo, 1982, 0 330 26752 3.

The author explains why she wrote the book — because she remembered that, in her teens, little information was available and this was positively unhelpful to her: hence the book, which is based on a questionnaire sent to teenagers asking for their views and for questions on sex. Subsequently Miriam Stoppard met many groups of young people for further discussion. These questions and comments are incorporated into the book.

Thus information and advice is given on a realistic basis, and the author states that "...teenage sexual values are not casual", a finding based on her researches and meetings. She is concerned that information helps young people to feel confident and to develop friendships and relationships, and not to use the information indiscriminately.

The text reads in a lively, conversational manner covering all aspects — body changes, relationships, feelings, oral sex, intercourse and contraception — and, as it is based on young people's perspectives, is geared exactly to their needs (though some adult users have found this difficult to accept).

TUCKER, Jenny (editor).
Just 17 Advice Book.
Virgin, 1987, (O/P).

Its unambiguous approach is clear — the *Just 17 Advice Book* gives practical common-sense advice which is untainted by value judgements and non-patronising in tone. The main thrust of the book is concerned with relationships and with being natural and realistic but also responsible. The enjoyment — and pitfalls — of sex are covered and biological information is well explained, as is sexual awareness (whether it be masturbation, periods or homosexuality). The section on contraception is exceptionally clear giving as it does the advantages and disadvantages of all the major forms of contraception. Abortion and sexual health are also included and an extremely comprehensive list of addresses for further help is appended. Using a journalistic format with one person each writing a section or chapter, the writers all adopt a house style with clearly-headed paragraphs and points. The *Just 17* label may indicate that this is a book for girls alone and while it rightly gives a positive and equal portrayal of female sexuality, the book is meant for both sexes.

WARD, Brian.
Sex and Life.
Macdonald, 1988, 0 356 15242 1.

This commences with a brief history, placing sex in relation to attitudes of religion, society, etc. Conception, pregnancy and birth are adequately covered as are sexual techniques.

A feature of the section on contraception is the detail given to the Pill but it must be noted that this book is now thirteen years old so latest information on contraception is not included. This applies to the section on hygiene and disease as there is no mention of AIDS; the same holds true for the booklist and list of organisations, appended to the book. Little attention is given to the emotional needs of people and the need to take responsibility for the information given is almost entirely biological.

WELLINGS, Kaye.
First Love, First Sex: a practical guide to relationships.
Thorsons, 1986, 0 7225 1233 3.

This book's coverage is wide-ranging with the accent on all aspects of relationships and therefore the sexual or biological aspect is seen in the context of the whole relationship. It deals with the images and impressions young people have (real life v. celluloid and glossy magazine images) and the consequent pressures upon teenagers.

As with other titles in this section, this covers body changes, sex organs and sexual practices, and contraception. Unusually for a book of this type, the problem of age in relationships is tackled as are married/single partners, same-sex relationships, class, religion, racial origin, sexual abuse and it addresses the question of marriage or living together. Throughout, it gives very clear information and sound advice while asking the reader to think about the implications of the actions s/he may be contemplating.

In particular, Wellings is good on anti-stereotyping homosexuality (ie. not presented as an illness) while not promoting it. However, it was published too early to be useful for AIDS, and although there is very little on 'the family' in the book, it does argue for marriage. Indeed the title promotes discussion and thoughtful decision-making on all aspects of sexual relationships. The text reads well, is typographically well produced and is supported by good graphics and extensive use of quality illustrations.

WESTON, Carol.
Girl Talk: all the things your sisters never told you.
Pan, 1987, 0 330 29669 8.

This deals with a wide range of issues and experiences which occur in adolescence. While pointing out that girls do not have a monopoly on anxiety about their bodies, the author does encourage the reader to be smug about the 'girl talk' syndrome. The book is aimed at the female reader and provides comprehensive information and common-sense advice on a wide range of issues including body care, relationships, sex, drugs and education. The book virtually assumes a heterosexual relationship throughout and although giving the reader a good self-image of her own body and being aware of society's pressures/sex role expectations, nevertheless the overall impression is that the girl should present herself in the best light to be attractive to a boy.

The text, originally published in the United States, has been revised for use in this country, but this has not been altogether well-matched as the reader switches from a middle-class, middle America style to the more factual content which represents the British input. However, practical information is presented and the text refers to the list of (British) addresses appended. Unfortunately, a booklist is not included but a quiz of options to everyday occurrences (eg. dating) is.

This is in the same mould as Hayman and Tucker (reviewed in this section) but does not succeed as well as either of those titles.

AIDS

AIDS

Pictorial Charts Educational Trust, T745, 1988.

A set of four charts and notes provides another way of looking at the basic facts connected with AIDS. It leads into specific information by looking at viruses and how they can be transmitted, and then applies this to AIDS.

The last chart looks at safe sex and shows sexual intercourse where the man is wearing a condom.

The use of brash cartoon-style illustrations may not appeal totally to the intended age group and could result in hilarity in group situations where a mood of seriousness is wanted! Nevertheless, it will certainly help as a resource for use on Personal and Social Education courses in schools. The notes provide back-up information and a list of suggested questions for group discussion.

AIDS — what everybody needs to know.
Health Education Authority, 1987, STD 24, 0 903652 71 4.

An eighteen page leaflet which gives necessary information, couched in readable and non-emotive language. It is well set out with subtle use of graphics and concludes with a list of clinics and other helpful organisations.

Single or multiple copies of the leaflet are available.

BEVAN, Nicholas.
AIDS and Drugs.
Franklin Watts, 1989, 0 86313 779 2.

A comprehensive survey of relevant information on HIV and AIDS, which covers not only the biological aspects but also drugs and sex and the state of medical research into a vaccine for AIDS. The final section advises what to do if the reader is worried about AIDS.

The layout is clear with judicious use of photographs and diagrams and the vocabulary used makes a readable text without being simplistic. Useful appendices — a glossary and list of helpful organisations — are included as is an index. One small point mars the quality of the production however as the first chapter is on AIDS and drug abuse *followed* by a chapter entitled 'What is AIDS?' which seems an illogical arrangement even in a book entitled *AIDS and Drugs*.

CARNE, C. A.
AIDS.
BMA, 1987, 0 7279 0144 3.

This is strictly correct in its use of medical terms but for all that it is also relatively easy to read.

In brief sections, it looks at the incubation period of the virus, the origin and spread of HIV, high risk groups, symptoms and disease, the anti-HIV antibody test and treatment of AIDS and HIV. It also includes some illustrations of HIV and Karposi's Sarcoma.

This, then, seeks to explain the medical aspects of HIV to the general reader and may not be the necessary information a person who has AIDS requires. However, the booklet concludes with a useful list of addresses from which help may be obtained.

COLLIER, Caroline.
The 20th century plague.
Lion, 1987, 0 7459 1453 5.

Copyrighted to the Christian Medical Fellowship, this naturally takes a Christian viewpoint and while including medical and statistical information it looks at AIDS as a plague. This conception of AIDS as a plague feeds into myths and stereotyping and obscures the subject rather than giving useful information about it. The book propounds a Christian lifestyle as one, if not *the*, solution though it does argue for education about AIDS and help and support for AIDS sufferers.

DANIELS, V. G.
AIDS Questions and Answers.
Cambridge Medical Books, 1987 (2nd edition), 0 948920 84 X.

All aspects of AIDS are comprehensively answered in sixty questions on the subject, designed for the general reader. The author, a doctor, has researched his book over a good deal of time and includes not only medical aspects but also psychological and societal points as well as giving useful statistical information. A glossary, a detailed list of (regional) addresses of relevant agencies and a full index make this a helpful item when detailed information on AIDS is required.

HARVEY, Ian and REISS, Michael.
AIDSFACTS: educational material on AIDS for teachers and students.
Cambridge Medical Books, 1987 (2nd edition), 0 948920 06 8.

The aim of this pack of thirty A4 sheets is to support teaching of AIDS to 13 – 19 year olds. It makes the point that many other materials should be used and the pack incorporates a good deal of information, both biological and societal (with many graphs and with statistics to May 1987) and sheets for group discussion and exercises. The aspects covered include safer sex and condoms, the moral dimension and how to cope with AIDS. A list of books and other teaching materials is included, although most is of an advanced level. The sheets can be photocopied for classroom purposes and as such can be effectively used in a course of study.

HAWKES, Nigel.
AIDS.
Franklin Watts, 1987, 0 86313 628 1; 0 86313 632 X.

While written during a climate of panic and representing the illness as largely a homosexual disease, this book nevertheless effectively gets over the facts to its intended readership. Using the now accepted house style of the *Issues* series — good marriage of clear print, accessible text, apt illustrations, colour and graphics — the information and issues connected with HIV and AIDS are set out and provide the reader with pointers with which to discuss and give further thought to the issue.

HIV and AIDS BULLETIN.
(no 4 – Jan. 89) (irregular).
YOUTH MATTERS (68 Charlton St LONDON NW1 1JR 01-388 0241).

This contains examples of students' own work — posters advocating safe sex and the dangers of AIDS — and so it provides the perspective of young people themselves. It appears to have the cooperation of the Terrance Higgins Trust and the covering note to the bulletin suggests uses for this work ie. either photocopied (the producers require permission to be obtained before photocopying) or as a starting point for discussion.

A large-print version of the bulletin is also available.

KILPATRICK, David and Alison.
AIDS.
Chambers, 1987, 0 550 20571 3.

An accessible text but also one which is patronising and moralistic in places. It gives detailed biological data among other information but this is not always relevant or useful to its intended readership. It is also very weak on prevention and safe sex and ultimately helps rather than hinders stereotyped images of the disease and its sufferers and reproduces rather than allays fears of AIDS.

LERNER, Ethan A.
Understanding AIDS.
Lerner, 1987, 0 8225 0024 8.

For younger children, this aims to provide enough information and advice to enable them to understand AIDS. It describes factually and simply HIV, ARC and AIDS and, through fictionalised stories of people who have and do not have AIDS, looks at the feelings and emotions people experience. The climate of panic is clearly seen in the book, as in the sections on a haemophiliac child who has AIDS through an infected blood transfusion and a boy who is subsequently found to have appendicitis although it is rumoured he has AIDS.

While the book does acknowledge AIDS is now likely to be caught by heterosexuals, AIDS is seen primarily as a gay disease. Although the author tries to be fair in explaining homosexuality, it is mainly presented as an adolescent stage to be passed through.

An interesting book but one which does not work especially when allied to the very specific (and somewhat twee) Americanisms used and the dull illustrations which will not find a rapport with British readers.

LOVE CAREFULLY: use a condom.
BROOK Advisory Centres (leaflet).

An A4 folded sheet, with good graphics, simply advocates the use of condoms to mitigate against the effect of AIDS. Melanie McFadyean of *Just 17* magazine gives a brief introduction to advocate the use of condoms in loving carefully. A checklist is also included as well as a list of telephone numbers of helpful organisations.

ROUAN, Christopher.
Understanding AIDS: a self-defence manual.
Ryburn, 1987, 1 85331 001 8.

The author gives detailed medical information about HIV and AIDS, much of which will not be helpful or relevant to the intended readership. The disease is seen as one which can be contracted by many sexually-active people, not only homosexuals and so it dispels myths and deals with the emotional needs of AIDS sufferers and of those caring for people with AIDS. The book advocates monogamy and rather grudgingly gives information on condoms and safer sex.

The use of much medical terminology and details counteracts the intention of the book for the reader to understand AIDS and there is no indication that further advice/help may be found elsewhere.

WACHTER, Oralee.
Sex, drugs and AIDS.
Penguin, 1987, (O/P).

This aims to ally fears and panic, to present an accurate portrayal of AIDS and its sufferers and to give sensible advice on how not to get AIDS. It succeeds in doing all this for it clearly states how AIDS is and is not caught, shows that the virus and disease is not principally a homosexual one but one that can be caught by any sexually-active person, as well as drug users, and gives practical advice on using condoms and safe sex.

First published in the United States, it accompanies a video of the same title and clearly the photographs used in the book are direct from the video which would account for the poor reproduction. It is designed to have street credibility as it includes presentations from pop stars and personalised information is given direct. The text is very simple — in layout and reading level it appears similar to the old 'reluctant reader' series of a decade ago.

An appendix, provided by the Terrance Higgins Trust, provides further information about the disease.

WILKINSON, Graham.
Let's discuss AIDS.
Wayland, 1987, 1 85210 295 0.

This looks at medical aspects of HIV and AIDS, its history and development; similarly, the effects on both sexes and society's attitudes are examined.

Safe sex, drug abuse, education and government policies provide a wide range of aspects but the book does present the illness as mainly a gay one.

Five case studies show a variety of responses from sufferers and others and these allow the reader to think about and discuss particular issues and come to some decisions which bear on their own behaviour and lives. These case studies are not subject to copyright and may be copied for use in the classroom.

The illustrations include contemporary photographs and reproduced government publicity/posters giving warnings about AIDS.

CHILD SEXUAL ABUSE

Child Sexual Abuse

This was, until recently, a topic ignored by sex education (as by society at large) but over the last few years a number of titles have become available which attempt to deal with the issue. It is a very sensitive area and books are welcome which fulfil one or more of the main needs:

SEX EDUCATION NEEDS AND APPROACHES
1. Educating all young people in 'saying no', in safe and unsafe touching, in looking after themselves. This area is concerned with self respect and the development of autonomy, not merely with information.
2. Helping young people who may have suffered abuse to talk about it.
3. Helping adults in developing approaches to the subject with young people.

SELECTION CRITERIA
* Does the text manage to educate towards safety without making a child feel unsafe, that all contact with adults is risky, that the world is too dangerous a place?
* Does the text merely talk about the dangers of strangers, rather than of contact with family members?
* Does the text help children to find ways of talking about it to others and provide sources of practical help, outside the family if necessary?

BALDWIN, Dorothy and LISTER, Claire.
Safety when Alone.
Wayland, 1987, 1 85210 083 4.

Text which is easy to read and understand takes a young child through the reasons why s/he should take precautions and follow a safety code when alone. This is done in a societal context and thus manages to give reassurance to children as well as clearly warning them of potential danger.

'Personal space' is well explained and provides a framework to discuss hugs and kisses and then looks at 'private places' ie. areas of the body which may be in danger from 'touching games'.

Throughout, the book gives clear advice on what children should do if in any danger and a list of safety rules are appended. The Royal Society for the Prevention of Accidents assisted the publishers with the book and the good clear print and photographs, which show a multi-cultural society, marry well and provide a title which can be read by young children themselves and by professionals in particular circumstances.

Age: 4 – 7.

BENEDICT, Helen.
Safe, Strong and Streetwise — the teenage survival guide.
Hodder & Stoughton, 1988, 0 340 42966 6. (also available in paperback — 0 340 48495 0).

In spite of its title, this seeks to set a perspective of ordinary life, but urges the reader to be aware of sexual assault. It looks in detail at sexual assault, eg. how it happens, who is a rapist, street harassment, etc. The text specifies an individual's sexual rights and responsibilities. Also covered is how to protect oneself, including detailed points on particular situations eg. on dates, in work. There is advice on safety at home, such as how to handle break-ins, obscene 'phone calls, safety in school and while babysitting.

A section deals with self-defence and there is a detailed list of sources of safety. The book claims to deal with an area of sexual assault still taboo, ie. male sexual assault, whether heterosexual or homosexual, but does so in a way which is sensitive to and acknowledges the rights of gay people. Finally, there is a section for parents, to help with situations where their children have been sexually assaulted.

The solid text is little broken-up by illustration and whilst it is practical, fairly easy to read and has little Americanisms (it was first published in the United States), information retrieval is hindered by the absence of an index. A good up-to-date resources list is, however, appended.

Age: 14 + .

DAY, Roger.
Hands Off!.
Harvestime, 1987, 0 94771 422 7.

This is a story of a boy who is sexually abused by his uncle and, although ashamed of this, does not tell his parents. When the uncle goes to prison for sexually assaulting someone else, the boy feels guilty. This guilt grows and causes great pressure. The way out in this story is to tell his story to the preacher of an evangelical non-conformist denomination. It transpires that there had been a history of sexual abuse in the family which caused the problem his uncle faces. However, the boy is encouraged to forgive his abuser. The story is confusing and the whole narrative misses the age range for which it is intended, uses stereotyped characters and would not seem to hold the attention or help any reader who has experienced sexual assault.

This is written from a specifically Christian point of view and is evangelical in tone. Whilst faith does have a role to play, there is little mention of any agency or professional to which a child may turn to for help, save a passing reference to Childline, and certainly no list of helpful addresses, telephone numbers, etc.

Age: 13 + .

ELLIOTT, Michele.
The Willow St Kids — It's your right to be safe.
Andre Deutsch, 1986, 0 233 97954 9.

Using an imaginary primary school setting, stories are presented to illustrate different aspects of how children's safety can be violated (eg. flashing, touching); however, the stories offer good guidance to children in what to do as they follow a class of children through the school year in a well-written and easy-to-read text.

The book, which is recommended by Kidscape, whose director is the author, concludes with a list of helpful addresses for children to contact, and a postscript of relevant advice for adults.

Age: 8 – 11.

HESSELL, Jenny.
What's wrong with bottoms?
Hutchinson, 1987, 0 09 173536 X.

A picture-book like format is utilised to convey a child's feelings of sexual abuse by her uncle. The story is simply and clearly told with the child doing all the correct things (after an initial promise not to reveal anything to her parents) ie. telling her mother. The mother acts very responsibly and tries to explain to the child why Uncle Henry's actions are wrong but it is rather coy here and one suspects a child will still be asking "why?" at the end of the book.

The vocabulary does not read well in some places and it is a pity the father does not figure in the book. Nevertheless it is a useful, bibliotherapeutic item to use with small children who have experienced such situations.

Age: 5 – 6.

* Later published in paperback as I'm glad I told mum!
  Beaver, 0 09 959500 1.

LENNET, Robin and CRANE, Bob.
It's OK to say No!: A parent/child manual for the protection of children.
Thorsons, 1986, 0 7225 1328 3.

Short accounts of incidents which happen to young children are used in this book, each ending with a question asking what the reader would do if in the same situation. These are preceeded by a lengthy introduction for adults on the problems of child sexual assault and strategies for dealing with it. The title was originally published in the United States and, although the text is very easy to read, it is hindered by dated cartoon-like illustrations, printed on poor quality paper.

Age: 6 – 8.

PARK, Angela.
Child abuse.
Franklin Watts, 1988, 0 86313 778 4.

Briefly but effectively looks at aspects of child abuse, including incest, paedophile abuse and sexual exploitation. Also covered is how to recognise child abuse; case studies provide more detail and thought and the title looks too at both the victim and the abuser.

The text is in harmony with the illustrations and graphics and the textual level and length of the book will make it easily usable by a wide range of age and interest groups, as well as for professional use by teachers and librarians.

Age: 12 – 15.

STONES, Rosemary.
Too Close Encounters and what to do about them: a guide for teenagers.
Magnet, 1987, 0 416 03162 2.

An extremely readable and concise book with a good deal of eminently sensible advice aimed at young people.

Not only does it give lists of practical points to bear in mind when in situations of sexual harassment, ranging from school, the street and babysitting, but it also looks at body and clothes language, for instance, and discusses why problems of unwanted sexual attention occur.

A comprehensive list of helpful organisations and a booklist of both fiction and non-fiction titles is appended.

Such a title should find a home in most teenage sections of public libraries, as well as school and college libraries, and is useful for professionals to develop approaches to the subject with younger age groups.

Age: 12 – 17.

TERKEL, Susan N. and RENCH, Janice E.
Feeling Safe, Feeling Strong: how to avoid sexual abuse and what to do if it happens to you.
Lerner, 1985, 0 8225 0021 3.

Short, fictional stories look at different aspects of sexual abuse, including pornography, exhibitionism, incest, obscene telephone calls and rape. At the conclusion of each story, points are made and questions asked of the reader. The final chapter is a statement of a child's human rights.

Although first published in the United States, the treatment of the topic is such that it will be useful in a general way in this country. The textual level is quite easy and the style and Americanisms will be familiar to those who have read contemporary American children's novels.

Age: 9 – 11.

WACHTER, Oralee.
No More Secrets for me.
Viking Kestrel, 1983, (O/P); Penguin, 1986, 0 14 031925 5.

Another title which uses the device of short stories to illustrate examples of sexual problems which children face today. All of the stories promote the point that children should communicate their fears to a reliable adult and not keep secrets to themselves.

A simple text is used and together with the good large size of print used, should allow a young child easy access to relevant information and comfort.

A brief list of helpful organisations is appended, as is a briefing note to parents and carers.

Age: 7 – 9.

MATERIALS FOR PARENTS, CARERS AND TEACHERS

Materials for Parents, Carers and Teachers

AIDS: some questions and answers — facts for teachers, lecturers and youth workers.
Dept of Education and Science/Welsh Office/Scottish Office and Northern Ireland Office.
HMSO, 1987 Dd, 8935510.

Brief and comprehensive answers are given to the most commonly-asked questions and include medical and statistical information on HIV, AIDS and ARC. It makes clear government policy and in particular its publicity campaign regarding AIDS.

A list of further reading, ie. official publications, is given, with individual national items, such as Welsh language publications, also listed.

ALLEN, Isobel.
Education in sex and personal relationships.
Policy Studies Institute, 1987, 0 85374 330 4.

A wide-ranging discussion and evaluation of sex education — both formal and informal — based on a survey of a number of teenagers in 1985 and their parents. It looked at the sex education these teenagers had in both primary and secondary schools, the content, understanding and effect and the parents expectations and role in this.

Detailed investigation into the strategies for delivering such a curriculum is seen in the report. Other factors include the influence of friends and peer groups and also of the media. As important in terms of this list is the chapter on teenagers' sources of information on sex, contraception and personal relationships, as well as an assessment of the major sources of information.

Teenagers' own assessment, and that of their parents, of the education and influences these teenagers received together with a discussion on whose responsibility it is to ensure young people receive adequate instruction and information, a look at the survey's findings and a number of recommendations will provide helpful information for those educators and resource providers, in both primary and secondary sectors, to evaluate or re-think their aims, coverage and provision.

CATHOLIC MARRIAGE ADVISORY COUNCIL.
Choosing marriage;
Why wait for marriage;
Unborn but alive.
Think about it...leaflets (A4) from Catholic Marriage Advisory Council, Service for Teachers, Clitherow House, 1 Blythe Mews, Blythe Rd, LONDON W14 0NW (01 371 1341).

The texts are brief and chatty in tone and present a Catholic view on marriage, sexual intercourse and abortion.

Choosing marriage looks at the reasons for marriage and marriage for life, and throughout propounds the need and desire for a loving, caring relationship by both partners.

Why wait for marriage? looks at the power and responsibility of being 'sexually grown up'. Contraceptives are briefly and simplistically looked at, but the Church's teaching and, again, the need for real and lasting loving relationships is seen as vital.

Unborn but alive focusses on the early development of the foetus as a 'potential human being', the need or otherwise for abortion, the legal position and what the individual should do. (The leaflet refers several times to *Life*.)

These information sheets are part of a service to teachers and can be used for discussion purposes.

DAVIES, Mary.
Sex education for young people with a physical disability: a guide for teachers and parents.
Assoc. to aid the sexual and personal relationships of the disabled (SPOD), 0 9509786 0 4.

Aimed at parents and teachers, this booklet details the enhancements needed for existing sex education programmes to show and explain sex and sexual activity for the physically handicapped. The effects of physical disabilities on sexual functions are described and advice is given on overcoming practical problems, such as menstruation. Suggestions for class/group work with young people are given where attitudes are discussed as much as practical help is given.

Appendices include a list of the effects of various disabilities on sexual activities and aids for handicapped people to help achieve an erection.

DEPARTMENT OF EDUCATION AND SCIENCE.
Health Education from 5 to 16 (Curricum Matters 6).
HMSO, 1986, 0 11 270592 8.

Issued as a discussion document, this suggests ways in which schools may implement a health education curriculum. It describes the trend away from traditional approaches (ie. hygiene and sex education) towards a whole school context, with the aim of providing pupils with enough knowledge and skills to have good 'self esteem', and to make 'informed choices' and have a 'sense of responsibility'. As such, planning is vital and the report offers a framework for policy, planning and teaching strategies. It also includes a specific discussion of sex education.

Objectives are identified in both primary and secondary areas of education where, for instance, in secondary schools, the relevance of PSE courses and effectiveness through a whole curriculum approach are discussed. This HMI document is also more specific in that, for example, it points out the need to be sensitive to cultural diversity, with attendant home beliefs and values, of pupils. Also, the question of contraceptive advice to under 16's, STD and child sexual abuse are covered.

Finally, the document appends a list of supportive organisations, including the Schools Council Health Education Project (5 – 13; 13 – 18), health education officers, school library services, and advises on appropriate use of outside agencies.

DIXON, Hilary and MULLINER, Gill (eds).
Taught Not Caught: strategies for sex education.
Learning Development Aids, 1985, 0 905114 15 9.

First published in the United States, this British edition provides an astonishing array of techniques and content for those involved in sex education.

It advises on framing a course, preparation and techniques for teaching and learning as well as advice on resources and evaluation of courses.

Virtually every aspect of sex education is covered separately each with the following criteria: objectives, necessary preparation needed, optimum age group and group size, time needed for session, resources required, how to do it and possible variations. Quizzes and other prepared sheets are also provided. A most comprehensive list of resources and addresses of helpful organisations is appended but no index (though a detailed contents list is included).

ELLIOTT, Michele.
Keeping safe: a practical guide to talking with children.
New English Library, 1988, 0 450 43117 7.

First published in 1984 as *Preventing child sexual assault*,* this has been extended to cover other aspects of child safety as well as sexual assault, thus giving a better context. The text gives clear information and advice on handling cases of child sexual assault with children of all ages and teenagers. It sets child sexual assault in context, gives advice to teachers on formal lessons and child-contact, as well as more informal talks for parents and carers. Strategies for dealing with individual cases of child sexual assault are shown as well as preventative techniques.

The text also covers drugs, AIDS, bullying and dangers in other societal settings, ranging from amusement arcades to pornographic videos. Elliott advises parents on the extent to which children will accept guidance and safety limits but advocates

---

* Available as an audio-cassette from the Royal National Institute for the Blind —
2 cassettes T5548/2.

communication and understanding by all parties. She says this preventative approach is an on-going one and that one should not be complacent just because more and more schools and agencies are child-safety conscious and are developing preventative teaching programmes.

The author gives excellent information and practical advice on talking and working with teenagers as well as children, and appends questionnaires to use with different age groups, as well as an admirable list of sources of help and an annotated resource list.

Only one point mars a most helpful item: the lack of an index — although the detailed contents list helps.

GREENGROSS, Wendy.
Sex and the handicapped child.
National Marriage Guidance Council, 1980, 0 85351 051 2.

Aimed at parents and carers of handicapped children, this looks mainly at the change in attitudes needed to allow disabled young people to participate in sexual activity. The text discusses and argues the case for sexual independence quite clearly and advocates that parents look for counselling and advice in order to help their children. It also points out that many organisations can help and provide factual information/publications and offer practical help. A detailed list of relevant addresses is appended, as is a list of recommended books.

I NEVER TOLD A SOUL.
Brook Advisory Centres, 1986, tape + booklet.

A discussion with Julie who was 14/15 years of age when she first had intercourse and became pregnant. She did not tell anyone until she was seven months pregnant.

The detailed and helpful teaching notes suggest strategies for group discussion as well as follow-up work.

Recommended reading for tutors is also given as is a transcript of the cassette.

MADARAS, Lynda.
What's happening to my body?: a growing-up guide for parents and daughters.
Penguin, 1989 (2nd edition), 0 14 008822 9.
What's happening to my body?: a growing-up guide for parents and sons.
Penguin, 1989 (2nd edition), 0 14 008823 7.

In both titles, the author collaborates with a teenager of the relevant sex to provide a youth perspective. The titles are prefaced by a lengthy introduction to parents encouraging them to communicate and inform their children, and to provide opportunities and encouragement for their children to ask questions. The remainder of the texts is written in a straight-forward easy-to-read manner, in which the majority of the data presented is medical and each title provides information on the bodily development of the other sex. This information is mostly relevant (though with too much detailed medical input at times — bearing in mind that these texts are aimed at younger teenagers) and indeed promotes good self-image for both sexes. It purports to 'promote discussion' but it would need a very confident parent for the text is full and seemingly complete — indeed, as the book also suggests, this text/format would be more helpful to a teacher who could use it in a formal setting and who may be better prepared to promote discussion.

The text includes all the aspects of pubertal development, sexual intercourse, reproduction, contraception and sexually transmitted diseases. The text infers a familial setting and, although homosexuality is covered in a balanced manner, a heterosexual relationship is assumed. While responsibility by both partners for their actions/decisions is advocated when covering contraception, a look at the emotional and relational aspects is divorced from the text, for this is treated quite separately at the end of the books.

While noting the author's aim in writing separate texts for each sex, this seems as much a publishing accident in that they were originally published in the United States in 1983 and 1984, so it would be more helpful to have amalgamated both titles for much of the text is reproduced in each title as indeed it should be.

The photographic cover for the boys' title suggests a younger age than the book is intended for, but otherwise the typographical production is to a good standard and although supplied with an excellent index, no appendices are provided (but it must be noted that telephone numbers of helpful organisations and agencies are referred to in the texts.)

This would seem to be of more limited use than other titles reviewed earlier, such as Llewellyn-Jones and Wellings.

MAYLE, Peter.
Where did I come from?
Virgin video, WC 181 PG (VHS), 1986. Consolidated Distribution Ltd.

Based on the book of the same title by Peter Mayle (reviewed earlier) this uses animation in an amusing way to explain conception and birth. Johnny Morris' narration provides gentle humour and information in a simple but clear way: however, the video is very coy about showing sexual intercourse. The music is somewhat banal and intrusive and the lengthy opening sequence shows stereotyped racial characteristics. Its use could only effectively be with young children.

NATIONAL COUNCIL OF WOMEN OF GREAT BRITAIN.
Sex Education — whose responsibility?: Report by a working party of the National Council of Women of Great Britain, including the results of a survey of 81 schools.
NCWGB, 1984.

This working party was set up in 1982 to enquire into material used for sex education in schools. The report looks at the background of official reports and guidelines, contemporary data, and then at the role of parents, the community and LEAs. Strategies in evolving relevant lessons are examined as are resources and the role of teachers in evaluating such items. This is seen as vital as is the apt use of resources in schools. Morality and the need for understanding and discussion is another feature of the report as is the necessity for adequate training of educators.

The report concludes with recommendations, including the vital necessity for a relevant form of social and personal development to include 'sex education and education about parenthood', the role of explicit information, the role of the Head and that of parents, and the need for a relevant and workable policy were also propounded.

This will provide many points of reference and questions to help educators look at their aims and objectives in establishing, maintaining and monitoring a sex education curriculum, in which the role of information and resources plays a constituent part.

NILSSON, Lennart.
A Child is born.
Faber, 1977, 0 571 11139 4.

A revised and translated edition, first published in the 1960's in Sweden. It incorporates many colour and black and white photographs of the stages of pregnancy and birth. Aimed at parents, it includes much relevant biological information for this post-conception stage for both parents and the as yet unborn child. Aspects of pregnancy, such as medical care, haemorrhoids, leg cramps and prenatal exercise are also included.

PICKERING, Lucienne.
Parents Listen.
G. Chapman, 1981, 0 225 66311 2.

This gives advice and strategies for coping with situations which many parents find embarrassing such as explaining the facts of life to their offspring from toddlers to teenagers.

The author discusses attitudes, ways to develop conversation and how to handle specific situations eg. masturbation, homosexuality, rape, teenage mothers, divorced parents, etc.

The basic tenet is communication and this title is infinitely superior to its companion titles *Boys talk* and *Girls talk* reviewed earlier.

Unfortunately there is no index nor appendix giving useful information such as addresses, etc.

PROHIBITION ON PROMOTING HOMOSEXUALITY BY TEACHING OR BY PUBLISHING MATERIAL.
The Library Association, 1988.

This reproduces the text of *Clause 28* and goes on to describe possible implications of the Act, including the pressure by various groups or individuals for librarians to censor their stock. This brief is to provide staff with 'defensive material', ie. quotes from debates in Parliament, to counter any such proposition.

Extensive quotes from the Minister for the Arts and the Minister of State at the Home Office are given as is the amendment as proposed by the Library Association.

An appendix gives Hansard references to debates on this clause.

As such, it will be useful to be aware of this item and certainly to know of its whereabouts in a given library authority.

PROTECT YOUR CHILD: a guide about child abuse for parents.
NSPCC.

An admirably practical leaflet which sets out in point form the varieties of abuse which occur, offers advice on sexual abuse such as looking for signs, helping the child tell the parent and coping with a partner who is abusing a child, who to tell and what the law says.

SEX EDUCATION AT SCHOOL.
DES, Circular No 11/87, 1987.

This draws together the physical and emotional needs of young people in terms of 'appropriate and responsible sex education' in schools. It looks at the need for policy and the role of governors, parents, heads, teachers and LEAs.

How to cover this area in a 5 – 16 curriculum is examined. The circular considers the maturity of the pupil and sensitivity in teaching approaches are keynotes here and content (and thus resource provision and advice) should not just reflect the chronological age groupings.

The circular also makes reference to the situation in special schools, the moral framework, AIDS and advice to pupils under 16 years.

SHENNAN, Victoria.
Help your child to understand sex.
National Society for Mentally Handicapped Children & Adults, 1976, 0 855 37039 4.

The author gives an individual viewpoint and looks at possible changes of attitude and/or extra skills needed in order to explain sex to handicapped children and young people and set it in the context of a perfectly ordinary activity for people to engage in.

However, on discussing homosexuality, the author takes the stance that mentally handicapped males may need to be aware of such activity and 'need to have enough knowledge to protect themselves against such advances': so the premise is that mentally handicapped males may not be homosexuals themselves.

WARREN, Hugh.
Talking about School.
London Gay Teenage Group, 1984, 0 9509455 2 8.

This title follows on from *Something to tell you: the experience and needs of young lesbian and gay men in London* (1984) and is aimed at those who work in the education system. Its aims are to argue that information is needed on homosexuality in schools and that accepted and negative attitudes are harmful and should be changed. It examines stereotyping and the life of young homosexuals and lesbians at school, basing some of its views on the findings of a questionnaire for *Something to tell you*. Generally, it advocates greater availability of information in schools and examines the responsibility of various groups (teachers, LEAs etc.), to be aware of the needs of young people. In particular it gives detailed strategies for developing the curriculum to accommodate courses on homosexuality and argues that teachers need to critically analyse current learning materials for bias. The role of homosexual and lesbian teachers is also discussed and the role of all staff, especially those involved with pastoral care, is covered. Appended is a large list of resources, particularly books (both fiction and non-fiction) divided into subject areas, eg. history, politics, law, sociology and English, plus a list of relevant organisations.

WENT, Dilys.
Sex Education: some guidelines for teachers.
Bell & Hyman, 1985, 0 7135 2468 5.

On the basis that teachers from many subject areas are now asked to take part in sex education lessons, this book aims to provide a fund of knowledge, strategies, advice on resources and where to seek further help.

It comprehensively covers nearly all relevant aspects of sex education, including puberty, the range of human sexuality, gender, contraception, health care, menstruation, family planning, abortion, STD, marriage and morality. The emotional and relational aspects are seen as vitally important and the book stresses that sex education must be taught in context. While specific issues are dealt with separately, the book treats three age groups distinctly: 0 – 8; 9 – 13; 14 – 18. Went looks at the aim of the sex education curriculum for these age ranges and the particular elements to be drawn out. For example, in planning a course for the first group, the author advises looking carefully at the vocabulary needed and the strategies to use. She also provides common questions which pupils may ask and gives pointers on dealing with these in a comforting manner. This is all prefaced by a look at the role and context of sex education in schools and official guidelines (this preceeds the 1987 DES circular) and a detailed discussion on the role of parents (but not governors). The book does not deal with AIDS, nor rape, but briefly includes child sexual assault. Extensive lists of resources are given, most of which will be most helpful, although some caution is advised, eg. *Peter and Caroline* (1957), now extremely dated, is recommended and Jane Cousin's *Make it Happy* (1978) is not mentioned. Also, unhelpful parallels are drawn, eg. in an otherwise balanced discussion of homosexuality, statistics are given to the effect that three million people are gay, or 'equivalent to...the population of Wales (though not all Welsh people are gay!)'.

Nevertheless, the book does aim to ensure that young people should have enough information to make responsible decisions and have 'a good self-image and a positive outlook.'

WENT, Dilys.
Sex education in the curriculum (ACE information sheet).
Advisory Centre for Education, ACE Bulletin September 1987. (available as an information sheet from ACE, 18 Victoria Part Sq, LONDON E2 9PB).

Looks at the role of governors with the effects of the 1986 Education Act and other legislation in mind regarding sex education.

This brief information sheet gives detailed information on the duties of governors to decide policy, publish information and liaise with parents. Other aspects looked at include who is to teach this curriculum, the question of teaching in mixed or single-sex classes and what age sex education should begin.

Went provides the context of everyday school situations and advice in looking at morality, homosexuality and detailed aspects and implication of sex education in both primary and secondary sectors of education.

WHY IS IT FOR THEM AND NOT ME?
Video + presenter's pack, Brook Advisory Centre, 1984, ICV/169 VHS.

The video allows four adults with differing handicaps the opportunity to talk frankly about their upbringing and adolescence, their sex education experiences — or lack of — their need for this, and their feelings on first encountering a loving relationship involving sexual activity. The interviewer asks about their plans, hopes and happiness as well as problems they experience regarding sex, love and marriage.

Supporting material includes multiple copies of transcripts of the interviews and notes for the teacher/group leader, which provide points of discussion. These include highlighting and asking the group to consider the need for sex education for everyone, including handicapped people and the feelings of the handicapped when in the situations described on the video; other points include the need for help and information, support from and viewpoints of family and friends, and the importance of a handicapped person living as an integral member of society.

The video and notes set the need for sex education in the context of total life fulfilment and these resources can be used by many groups, whether as part of the sex education curriculum, or as a part of a social education programme.

APPENDIX: LIST OF ORGANISATIONS AND AGENCIES

The following provided information and material for research in this booklist, some of which are included in the body of the work. (This is not an exhaustive list, but several of the titles reviewed indicate if a comprehensive list of organisations is appended, and these should be approached for fuller information.) It should be noted that not all organisations publish their own material but some act as an umbrella organisation for smaller groups or to stock commercially-produced material.

The Association to Aid the Sexual and Personal Relationships of People with a Disability (SPOD)
286 Camden Road
LONDON N7 0BJ   Tel: 01 607 8851/2
Low-priced leaflets and information; also resource lists.

Brook Advisory Centres
Education and Publication Unit
24 Albert St
BIRMINGHAM B4 7UD   021 643 1554
Annual publications catalogue and leaflets on birth control for young people

Catholic Marriage Advisory Council,
Clitheroe House,
1 Blythe Mews
Blythe Rd
LONDON W14 0NW   01 371 1341
Detailed booklist with low-priced leaflets and books.

Department of Education and Science
Library
Room 2/69
Elizabeth House
York Rd
LONDON SE1 7PH   01 934 9139
Library bibliography No 82: sex education. October 1986. Unannotated list of books for use with children, books for teachers and periodical articles.

Family Planning Association
Education Unit
27 – 35 Mortimer St
LONDON WC1N 7RJ   01 636 7866
Leaflets, packs, information and booklist.

Health Education Authority
Hamilton House
Mabledon Place
LONDON WC1H 9TX   01 631 0930
Publications catalogue from above address; order individual items direct from local
health education unit.

KIDSCAPE
82 Brook St
LONDON W1Y 1YG   01 493 9845
Leaflets and information on child sexual abuse.

LIFE: save the unborn child
118 – 120 Warwick St
LEAMINGTON SPA   Warks.   CV32 4QY   0926 421587/311667
Series of specific and pro-active leaflets on broad Christian objections to abortion;
also booklist, posters and videos.

Marie Stopes House
108 Whitfield St
LONDON W1P 6BE   01 388 0662
London and regional centres provide information and leaflets on birth control.

Marriage Guidance Council (Relate)
Bookshop
Herbert Gray College
Little Church St
RUGBY   Warks.   CV21 3AP   0788 73241/60811
Catalogue with a wide-spanning list of publications.

MENCAP: Royal Society for Mentally Handicapped Children & Adults
123 Golden Lane
LONDON EC1Y 0RT   01 253 9433
General booklist and specific list on sex education books.

National Children's Bureau
8 Wakley St
LONDON EC1V 7QE   01 278 9441
Information and leaflets, including a list of materials and services about sex
education.

Terrance Higgins Trust
BM/AIDS
LONDON WC1 3XX   01 242 1010
Low-priced leaflets with specific information on HIV/AIDS.

AUTHOR INDEX

TITLE INDEX

Printed in Great Britain by Avon Litho Limited, Stratford-upon-Avon, Warwickshire, CV37 9NF.